Praise for CREATED EQUAL

"CREATED EQUAL is a book that speaks truth to power and is so very needed in today's divided society. Dr. Carson's sensible solutions and advice should be heeded by all Americans who wish to see our nation united once again."
—Dr. Alveda King, founder of SpeakForLife.org

"Ben and Candy Carson's CREATED EQUAL offers a well-reasoned, calm, and thoughtful contribution to the often-polarized discussions of race in America. After acknowledging the pain and complexity of America's racial past, the Carsons address the present and the future of race relations in America. Instead of despair and finger-pointing, readers are left with a cause for optimism about America's future."
—Dr. Carol M. Swain, senior distinguished fellow for constitutional studies at the Texas Public Policy Foundation

"Dr. Carson's life story proves that through the promises of America, and consistent hard work, we are not destined to be defined by our challenging circumstances, but rather can pursue happiness and exhaust our potential as was intended by our Creator."
—John Rich, singer and songwriter

"He's done it again! Ben Carson has written another great book that sheds light on an important subject. Not only have his gifted hands been used to bring healing to many, but his service to America has also brought a perspective that has the potential of bringing unity to what has been too long a divide across our nation."

—Franklin Graham, president and CEO of the Billy Graham Evangelistic Association and Samaritan's Purse

"Especially timely for our deeply polarized era, Dr. Carson's eloquent voice and commonsense perspective are more important than ever in pointing the way forward for all Americans of good will."

—Judge Ken Starr, former president and chancellor of Baylor University

"To the great number of Americans who care about the erosion of belief in American exceptionalism, add CREATED EQUAL to your reading list. Not because you will agree with every point Dr. Carson makes, but because his point of view—borne of a lived experience in realizing his American dream via personal excellence—sparks the type of spirited discourse our country needs to hear right now."

—Cordell Carter, Esq., executive director of the Aspen Institute Socrates Program

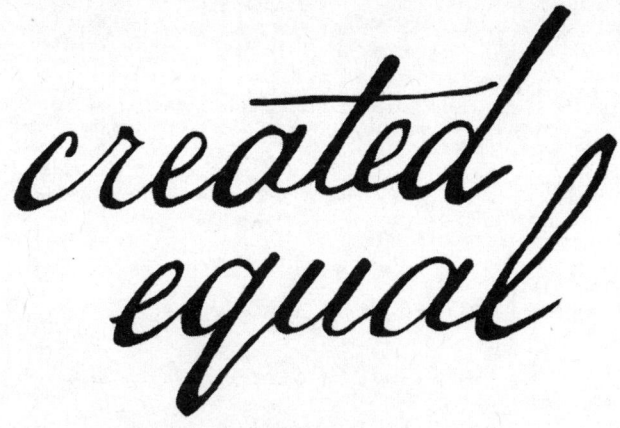

created equal

THE PAINFUL PAST, CONFUSING PRESENT, *and* HOPEFUL FUTURE OF RACE IN AMERICA

BEN CARSON, M.D.

with Candy Carson

Foreword by Dr. Alveda King

CENTER STREET

NEW YORK   NASHVILLE

The names and identifying characteristics of some individuals have been changed.

Copyright © 2022 by American Business Collaborative, LLC.
Foreword Copyright © 2022 by Dr. Alveda King
Cover design by Melissa Reagan. Cover copyright © 2022 by Hachette Book Group, Inc.

Benjamin S. Carson Sr. is represented by Yates & Yates, www.yates2.com.

Hachette Book Group supports the right to free expression and the value of copyright. The purpose of copyright is to encourage writers and artists to produce the creative works that enrich our culture.

The scanning, uploading, and distribution of this book without permission is a theft of the author's intellectual property. If you would like permission to use material from the book (other than for review purposes), please contact permissions@hbgusa.com. Thank you for your support of the author's rights.

Center Street
Hachette Book Group
1290 Avenue of the Americas, New York, NY 10104
centerstreet.com
twitter.com/centerstreet

Originally published in hardcover and ebook by Center Street in May 2022.
First Trade Edition: August 2024

Center Street is a division of Hachette Book Group, Inc.

The Center Street name and logo are registered trademarks of Hachette Book Group, Inc.

The publisher is not responsible for websites (or their content) that are not owned by the publisher.

The Hachette Speakers Bureau provides a wide range of authors for speaking events. To find out more, go to hachettespeakersbureau.com or email HachetteSpeakers@hbgusa.com.

Center Street books may be purchased in bulk for business, educational, or promotional use. For information, please contact your local bookseller or the Hachette Book Group Special Markets Department at special.markets@hbgusa.com.

All Scripture quotations are taken from the Holy Bible, King James Version (KJV), public domain.

All photos are courtesy of the author's personal collection.

Library of Congress Cataloging-in-Publication Data
Names: Carson, Ben, author. | Carson, Candy, author.
Title: Created equal : the painful past, confusing present, and hopeful future of race in America / Ben Carson, M.D., with Candy Carson.
Description: First edition. | New York : Center Street, 2022. | Includes bibliographical references. | Summary: "External physical characteristics that are genetically encoded are things over which no individual has control. But rather than appreciating the gift of diversity, some have chosen to use it to drive wedges between groups of people. Some of these external characteristics are associated with the past moral failing of slavery. Though slavery in America formally ended in the 1860s, the vestiges of that evil institution are still with us today, and those vestiges often inflict guilt on some and facilitate feelings of victimhood in others. In Created Equal, Dr. Carson uses his own personal experiences as a member of a racial minority, along with the writings and experiences of others from multiple backgrounds and demographics, to analyze the current state of race relations in America. Instead of using race as an excuse to remake America into something completely antithetical to the Constitution, Dr. Carson suggests ways to enhance and bring great success to our nation and all multiethnic societies by magnifying America's incredible strengths instead of her historical weaknesses"— Provided by publisher.
Identifiers: LCCN 2021059197 | ISBN 9781546002642 (hardcover) | ISBN 9781546002796 (ebook)
Subjects: LCSH: Racism—United States—History. | Equality—United States. | United States—Race relations. | United States—Social conditions.
Classification: LCC E184.A1 C3364 2022 | DDC 305.800973—dc23/eng/20220103
LC record available at https://lccn.loc.gov/2021059197

ISBN: 9781546002789 (trade pbk.), 9781546002796 (ebook)

Printed in the United States of America

LSC-C

Printing 1, 2024

This book is dedicated to the 1 percent of the American populace who volunteer for military service and to the first responders, both of whom protect the rest of us internationally and domestically every single day.

CONTENTS

Foreword   ix

CHAPTER 1   No One Is Born a Racist   1

CHAPTER 2   How We Look at Race   15

CHAPTER 3   The History of Slavery and Racism
            in America   35

CHAPTER 4   Guilt and Victimhood Surrounding
            Race   63

CHAPTER 5   Critical Race Theory and the 1619
            Project   83

CHAPTER 6   The George Floyd Turning Point   105

CHAPTER 7   Media and Big Tech   127

CHAPTER 8	Does Systemic Racism Exist in America?	147
CHAPTER 9	Judeo-Christian Values and Racism	169
CHAPTER 10	Is It Racism or Classism?	189
CHAPTER 11	Education, the Great Equalizer	209
CHAPTER 12	The Path Forward	229

Epilogue	249
Acknowledgments	251
Notes	253

FOREWORD

By Dr. Alveda King

Almost anyone across the political spectrum from the far left to the far right would probably agree with you that our country is in serious trouble and the divisiveness threatens not only peace, but our very existence. One of the areas of contention surrounds the concept of racial relationships.

This topic has taken center stage and serves as a linchpin for the argument that America is and always has been a racist nation.

As a result, we find ourselves in a situation where race is injected into an enormous number of our conversations. If not challenged, this premise of racial division fuels the easy—and wrong—conclusion that America is the worst place for Blacks and other minorities to live.

It is very disturbing that Black youth are being taught that they are inherently disadvantaged in our society and that no matter how hard they work these disadvantages will persist and preclude the realization of their potential. Equally as harmful is the pernicious indoctrination of white students, who are being taught to feel guilty about racially motivated injustices perpetrated by their ancestors. It is hard to imagine how teaching our children these divisive concepts can lead to a fairer and more peaceful society.

Yet, all hope is not lost. I have seen tremendous positive changes in our society during my lifetime. My uncle, Dr. Martin Luther King Jr., was a prophet and a preacher. Quoting from the Scripture in Acts 17:26–28, MLK acknowledged that God created one blood/one human race. He said: "What I'm saying today is that we must go from this convention and say, 'America, you must be born again!' Let us be dissatisfied until that day when nobody will shout, 'White Power!' When nobody will shout, 'Black Power!' but everybody will talk about God's power and human power."

After his death, MLK, notably as either a most loved or most hated public figure, became the first Black American after whom a national holiday was named. It's hard to imagine how that would happen in a systemically racist nation.

Yet this is not to say that we have not experienced severe racism in America during just this last century. We also cannot deny that racist principles have been inserted into our building blocks. For me, this reality marks a "wheat and tares" situation that must be weeded out with faith, hope, love, integrity, and intelligence—in every generation and every decade.

As William Cullen Bryant said, "Truth crushed to earth shall rise again." While this quote is credited to Cullen Bryant, and remains an inspiration to many, we may agree that Jesus says it best: "If you abide in my word, you are truly my disciples, and you will know the truth, and the truth will set you free" (John 8:31–32 ESV).

Through the years here in America, we have witnessed and, in some cases, experienced situations where Black people were relegated to the back of the bus or to separate railway cars and such treatment was enforced by legal authorities. Such practices have been tares in the foundations of our history.

Many have seen and, in some cases, experienced numerous situations where public and private services were refused for Black customers. We have seen and, in some cases, are still experiencing unfair lending practices and housing discrimination and segregation that has been enforced by unscrupulous legal authorities. While the list goes on and on, these are inherent tares in our system that can and must be weeded out.

Rather than dwell on these "tares" and complain about how unfair they were, and, in some cases, still are, we must build on the truth that many of these injustices have been largely defeated and relegated to the dustbins of history. In acknowledging the defeat of many racist policies erica, we must remember the lessons that have been learned: the good, the bad, and the ugly.

While not resting on any laurels, we must build upon the progress that has been made, decade by decade, generation by generation.

As one who is not just "talking the talk," Dr. Carson is "walking the walk" with us. He is throwing down a gauntlet. America, we have a choice to make. Do we harp and complain and cause disruptions because of the things that have happened in the past? Or do we build on the foundation of righteousness, truth, and justice, with the goal of defeating the horrible injustices of America's past?

The pathway of vengeance leads to further conflict and hatred. The path of truth with corresponding action leads to reconciliation and to further progress. Which side are we on? Please do not misconstrue what you read in this book to mean that we think racism is a thing of the past. Racism is alive and, in far too many instances, well today. As a result, we must continue to strive to obliterate racism in our society, in every decade and generation. Ignoring the tares, or resting on our laurels, would be a great disservice to our predecessors of all ethnic communities who sacrificed so much, including in some cases their lives to improve our society.

Why do we usually cheer for our sports team, regardless of the ethnic composition, over the team of our rivals, regardless of the ethnic composition? Does our behavior say something about how truly unimportant ethnicity is in the overall scheme of things? Is there any good thing that comes from the increasing racial animosity and division that is being cultivated by so many in our society today?

There is much confusion in America over race today because we haven't caught up with the scientific and spiritual truth: There is only one human race; skin color can denote ethnicity, not race.

In the past, and sadly sometimes here in the twenty-first century, we really don't have enough social interaction among human ethnicities. When we don't know each other, how can we reconcile as the human race?

When we turn a blind eye to the God-created gifts of ethnicity, including not just skin color but all of the cultural variations, we allow space for division among our communities.

Then the door opens for confusion, with certain people telling us that we are enemies, dividing us by the color of our skin. Today, why are we allowing our children to be pitted against each other and why are we tolerating people destroying neighborhoods that have been built by years of blood, sweat, and tears, based upon division by skin color, all in the name of racial equity?

Yet, hope is not lost. Do not despair because, as they say, "It's always darkest before the dawn." As this book will show, we the American people are not each other's enemies and with humility and caring for each other, from the womb to the tomb, the God-created and hopeful principles that established America will prevail.

* * *

Dr. Alveda C. King is the daughter of the late slain civil rights activist Rev. A. D. King and the niece of Dr. Martin Luther King Jr., and a Christian evangelist. Alveda is also a former Georgia state legislator, a college professor, a two-time presidential appointee, and a 2021 recipient of the Presidential Lifetime Achievement Award.

We hold these truths to be self-evident, that all men are created equal, that they are endowed by their Creator with certain unalienable Rights, that among these are Life, Liberty and the pursuit of Happiness.

The Declaration of Independence

CHAPTER 1

No One Is Born a Racist

ONE OF MY EARLIEST MEMORIES AS a small child was a family trip from Detroit to Chattanooga, Tennessee. The journey was made in the family car, a red-and-white Pontiac sedan. I can still remember seeing "white" and "colored" drinking fountains and lavatories. It was one of my most lasting and impactful memories from that trip. I was six years old and until that time had not been acutely aware of racial differences. However, in retrospect, there would have been no reason for me to concentrate on racial differences, because the world in which I moved did not have many of them. I lived in a Black neighborhood, attended Black schools, went to Black churches, and all of our friends and relatives were Black. My kindergarten teacher had been white and I saw white doctors and police officers fairly frequently, but they all seemed nice and non-threatening. Like many kids growing up in relative racial isolation, I had no reason to think about racial issues.

All of that changed when we moved to Boston. That move was occasioned by my parents' divorce when my mother discovered that her husband was a bigamist. They were both from Chattanooga, but my father was twenty-eight and my mother was thirteen when they got married and moved to Detroit looking for economic opportunity. She had less than a third-grade education but was very resourceful and wise. She saved every extra penny earned by my father as an assembly line worker and invested in property. At one point they had a substantial amount of property. I would have been born into very different circumstances if my father had not gambled away those resources and been engaged in other nefarious activities.

At any rate, my mother with her limited education was left with the task of trying to raise two young sons on her own, and we lacked an affordable home. Her sister and brother-in-law in Boston compassionately agreed to take us in. It was in Boston that I first encountered overt hostility based solely on race. I remember walking in Franklin Park and encountering a group of white adolescents who shouted racial obscenities at me and said, "Let's drown him," since we were near a body of water. I was quite fleet of foot and ran faster than I ever had in my life to escape them. I don't know if they would have really killed me, but I didn't want to find out.

A couple of my favorite older cousins were very friendly with, and probably were involved with, some of the drug dealers in the neighborhood. They frequently had run-ins with the police and often would come home battered and bloodied from those encounters. Needless to say, their versions of the confrontations would vary significantly with what the police had to say. But without question, the police officers we encountered in Boston were not nearly as nice as those in Detroit. This seemed to be based on racial tensions and the fact that we resided in a violent neighborhood with a lot of illegal activity.

Detroit, Chattanooga, Boston. Three different cities and three different environments with respect to racial tension. As you might imagine, people growing up in those different environments might have varying impressions about race in America. In the 1950s, Chattanooga was a typical southern city with the typical rules of segregation and societal interactions. It was the way things had always been and it afforded a false sense of peace and tranquility. When we were in Chattanooga, my parents and adult relatives were careful to explain the necessity of observing and complying with the signs indicating where you could relieve yourself and where you could drink. They said we wouldn't have to worry about that when we returned to Detroit. A mere decade later there were no longer such signs, and laws had been enacted against segregation and discrimination based on race, color, or national origin. In short, a great deal of racial progress had been made, although there was still a long way to go.

As a child I accepted and went along with the rules, as did almost all the adults, both Black and white, leading to a false sense of harmony. In fact, many Blacks were quite resentful of the Jim Crow laws and many whites were fearful of change. Nevertheless, it was brave people from all racial backgrounds who courageously challenged those rules and were responsible for the tremendous changes that took place. Protests and demonstrations led to some tumultuous years in which that harmony was obliterated. I can remember as a nine-year-old sitting in the kitchen getting a haircut by my uncle William and watching the television. The pictures of attack dogs and fire hoses being used by the police to put down demonstrations are still vivid in my memory. I felt tremendous empathy for those being attacked, while I had less than charitable feelings toward those doing the attacking. Obviously, this had a subconscious impact upon the way I thought about racial differences, and obviously the scenes and the chaos that ensued impacted the way both Black and white adults thought about race thereafter. Those negative images influenced me to the extent that I began to recognize that there were differences between Blacks and whites, and I became aware of the fact that some people would regard me differently because of my color.

Boston was a very different kind of place. It was supposed to be a center of intellectual prowess and progressive politics. That said, there was a great deal of white ethnic diversity, which resulted in tensions between the various factions. Some of the same tensions that existed in Europe were transferred to the streets of Boston. Nevertheless, the differences between the white groups seemed to dissipate when it came to opposing the integration of their neighborhoods by Blacks. Whites were brought together by their hatred of Blacks, which no doubt was caused by ignorance and a lack of understanding due to the propagation of untruths. There were also many untruths about whites that circulated in Black communities.

The tension peaked in the 1970s with the emergence of proposals to integrate the public schools. Many of the whites who considered themselves to be liberal joined with others in their community to oppose busing Black children into their schools. Some of the protests were quite violent, and in one famous photograph an American flag on a staff was being used to threaten a Black lawyer with stabbing. This racial animosity was nothing new to Massachusetts, which was the first colony to legalize slavery. Public records indicate that slaves were introduced into the environment in 1641 from the Caribbean islands. With the termination of slavery in America, cities like Boston did not enact overt Jim Crow laws, but instead sanctioned de facto Jim Crow laws by maintaining strict segregation and ignoring public acts of racial hostility.

Detroit was quite similar to Boston in that there were no overt signs of racism, but there were systems in place to maintain the "purity" of neighborhoods and social facilities. Generally, there was not much turmoil if one or a few Blacks entered a white environment, but if substantial numbers attempted to integrate an area, the fangs of racism would quickly be revealed. When we returned from Boston to Detroit in 1961, we lived on the white side of the railroad tracks and therefore I attended Higgins Elementary School, where I was one of very few Black students. Having been very poorly educated while in Boston, I was a terrible student at Higgins, but the expectations for Black students were so low that no one saw that as a problem, with the exception of my mother. Interestingly, one group of students was placed in "special education" classrooms because they were disruptive and experienced learning difficulties. The vast majority of those students were Black. I would most likely have been placed in that classroom except for the fact that I was a very scrawny little kid who would probably have been killed (or at least that was the thinking of those in charge).

When eye examinations were conducted at the school, it was discovered that my eyesight was so poor that it could be considered a handicap. I obtained glasses and for the first time could actually see the blackboard. Before that eye exam, I didn't know that anyone could see the board. I quickly went from an F student to a D student, which made me very proud, even though the other students still continued to tease me about being a dummy. The white homeroom teacher was absolutely thrilled with my progress and was full of praise for me. But in retrospect, I realize that her expectations for me were so low that meager intellectual advances by someone like me were considered great achievements.

My white classmates were generally accepting of me, but clearly by that time in their lives, like me, they had already begun to recognize racial differences and establish racial hierarchies. I distinctly remember sitting in the classroom watching television because one of my classmates was being featured on a local television show highlighting science projects. I had anticipated that the next project on the show was going to be that of our classmate John and told the girl sitting next to me, whose name was Sally, that John would be next. Instead, the next project was that of a young Black man. Sally turned to me and said, "I ought to wring your neck," simply because I had mistakenly implied that John was Black. Was Sally a horrible racist person? Probably not. But like many others, she had been raised to believe that Blacks were intellectually inferior to whites. Interestingly, at the time I really didn't think anything of her comment, because that was the world we lived in and that was the way people thought. Sally was a nice person, but she obviously had some racist tendencies, which were not innate but had been instilled by the environment in which she was raised. I harbor no resentment toward Sally and others like her, and I hope and pray that she has changed with the times.

From the fifth grade until the second half of the eighth grade, I was the rare Black student in a white educational environment. During that time, I went from the worst student in the class to the best. Interestingly, I knew the same students throughout that entire period and they generally accepted my intellectual metamorphosis and actually reached a point where many of them would come to me seeking help with their schoolwork. On the other hand, many of the white teachers seemed amazed, hostile, or resentful of the fact that a Black student was achieving at levels higher than the white students. For example, when I was in the eighth grade at Wilson Junior High School, a special assembly was held at the end of each semester during which the student with the highest academic achievement would receive a special award. I had anticipated being that student since I had an A average in all of my classes. In those days a student would carry their report card to each class and the teacher would mark it and return it to them. I had all A's as I entered the last class, which was band. I was confident that I was going to get an A in band since I was an excellent instrumentalist. Instead, the "turkey" band teacher gave me a C in order to ruin my report card and my chances of receiving the award. To his great chagrin, band did not count and I still received the award. At the ceremony, one of the white teachers took the microphone and publicly chastised the white kids for allowing a Black kid from a very disadvantaged background to be number one. My white classmates, who had known me for several years and had witnessed my transformation, were rolling their eyes, making the crazy sign, and pointing at that teacher with embarrassment.

The racial attitudes of my classmates had evolved in a positive direction over the three and a half years in which they observed my academic progression. Because they personally knew me, they began to see me more as a person than as a Black person. This is one of the reasons why it is so important to create positive exposure experiences for our young people and not keep them isolated within one demographic group. If we are to have a functional yet diverse population, this is a very important concept to understand.

As difficult as it may seem, we also should try to look at the comments of that teacher from another possible perspective. Instead of being blatantly racist, she could have been implying that those students who come from two-parent homes and have certain social and economic advantages should achieve at a level higher than someone from a broken home who is a member of a racial minority and is suffering from dire poverty. At best, her comments still would have been highly insensitive, particularly with my family in attendance. This teacher was an art teacher who had previously displayed some of my artwork as examples of how students should pursue the creation of certain types of art. She had frequently praised me for my artistry in front of the other students. The point is that we should keep an open mind and not immediately condemn so many everyday occurrences as racist in origin.

As we discussed earlier, my young life was quite tranquil, with very little to worry about. I suspect, however, that if the adults in my environment had started telling me that there were other individuals who didn't look like me who were trying to come into our lives and disturb our peace and that these people were dirty and dangerous, it would have colored my perceptions of those people. And it would have instilled fear that would have been converted into prejudice and ultimately racism. As an added bonus, I would have been able to blame these people who were different for any problems that were difficult to solve and that were producing stress in my life. This is not the only pathway to prejudice and racism, but it is a common one. And, yes, Black people can be subject to the same fears and anxiety that produce untoward emotional outcomes and racism in white people. Indeed, Blacks can be racist too.

Babies and small children care about the color of one's skin about as much as they care about the color of one's clothing. They can, however, be conditioned to react to external stimuli like color. Whether it is operant or classical conditioning can be argued, but the unfortunate outcome is the production of individuals who react to external physical characteristics over which there is no control as opposed to evaluating the character of an individual, which can be controlled. Without the psychological overlays, this is exactly what Dr. Martin Luther King Jr. was talking about when he said he had a dream that one day his children would live in a society where they would be judged by the content of their character and not the color of their skin.

Do people who create home, school, recreational, worship, or work environments conducive to the internalization of racial stereotypes and negativity—which leads their children and others to adopt racist attitudes—do so intentionally? In many, if not most, cases I suspect that they would be much more careful about the atmosphere they were creating if they realized the negative impact it would have on their children and society as a whole. We all must come to the realization that people are not racist when they are born, that racism is a very bad thing, and that it is within our power to drastically alter the conditions that produce it. It is vitally important to realize that children invariably seek approval from the adults who care for them. They learn very quickly what to do and say to win the approval of their guardians. This has obvious benefits for them, and winning such approval results in significant positive reinforcement. This is why words of affirmation from an adult with oversight after a child has uttered racially inflammatory comments are harmful and should be avoided.

People with Marxist ideologies who knew the importance of influencing children early on, like Vladimir Lenin, had so much confidence in early influence that he said, "Give me four years to teach the children and the seed I have sown will never be uprooted."[1] And the Bible itself, in Proverbs 22:6, says, "Train up a child in the way he should go: and when he is old, he will not depart from it." Clearly the importance of early childhood influences has been well known throughout the history of mankind, and now is the time to take advantage of that knowledge to sow the seeds of love, respect, and true tolerance even for those with whom we disagree.

Interestingly enough, unlike many other organs of the body, the brain has not achieved full developmental maturation at birth. One of the reasons that newborn babies sleep for such a long time is that their brains are still rapidly developing and need those times of respite to facilitate cellular development and synaptic networking. In fact, cerebral maturation continues well into the twenties. It is during the time of brain maturation that an individual is most receptive to inputs that affect their self-image and character. One of the reasons we can do dramatic operations on the brains of children is that their brains manifest something we call plasticity. That means that portions of the brain can be retrained and recruited to take over functions that have been lost by damage or surgical removal of other parts of the brain. The most dramatic instances are when we undertake an operation known as cerebral hemispherectomy, in which half of the brain is removed or disconnected to combat intractable seizures. The other half of the brain assumes many of the functions of the lost hemisphere, leaving some of these children with only minor motor dysfunction. The point of this description is to demonstrate that there are actual neuroanatomical reasons that young children are so pliable and receptive and vulnerable to environmental input and to emphasize how important it is to make sure that input is the correct material.

Recently, some developmental "experts" have argued that even little babies can be racist. They base this on the fact that some white babies tend to prefer white faces over Black faces. This is very superficial reasoning and should be rejected outright. This is not an example of racism, but rather demonstrates the human tendency to prefer that which is familiar over that which is new. If that same white baby sees only Black faces early on, they will prefer and feel more comfortable with Black faces than white faces. One of the real problems we face as a society right now is preferring the opinion of "experts" over common sense. These experts have burdened us with things like critical race theory that divide people rather than bring them together. By telling people that babies are racist, they are pushing the narrative of systemic racism and the opinion that virtually all people of a certain racial makeup are oppressors and others are the oppressed. They want people to believe that certain people are inherently oppressive and that everything they do or create has the objective of maintaining their superior position in society. The alternative, and in my opinion preferable, position is that everyone is an individual and that their character is their most important defining feature. That character is defined not by external physical features but by the accumulation of life and environmental experiences as well as their belief system.

A lifetime has passed since my early experiences with racism in Detroit, Chattanooga, and Boston. Happily, the racial atmosphere in all those places and across the country has changed markedly during my lifetime. We now have racial diversity in public office, integrated neighborhoods, integrated schools, integrated churches, and significant diversity among the educated and professional classes in all of those cities. This is not to say that we have reached Nirvana, but it is to say that tremendous advances in obliterating racism have been made, contrary to the narrative put forth by many today that we have a systemically racist system and nothing has changed. Yes, racism still exists, but so does liberty and justice for all. Each of us has the opportunity to choose which things we want to emphasize.

CHAPTER 2

How We Look at Race

ONE QUESTION THAT HAS EXISTED AMONG every group of people since the beginning of recorded history is, where did we come from and how did we get here? Many believe that we were created by God in His image and after His likeness as is stated in the Bible. Others believe that we evolved after a mixture of chemicals and electric impulses stimulated life forces that eventually evolved into many complex species of animals, including humans. In either case, there was a common ancestor from which all the different races are derived. As people migrated to different parts of the world, they were impacted by different environments. For instance, those in hot, sunny climates did better with dark skin and therefore the progeny with darker skin had better survival rates and were able to procreate, thereby passing on the genetic characteristics that benefited them. The same kinds of changes were seen around the globe, with different results depending on the environment.

Even though the external physical characteristics differed depending on the environment, the important thing that all groups shared was a terrific brain with massive intellectual potential. This is what allowed survival even among savage beasts, and it is what allowed humankind to thrive and dominate the planet. That brain is also what allows us to recognize and respect each other and to cooperate as we build societal infrastructure and facilitate peaceful coexistence. However, that same brain can be programmed to hate others and to try to harm them or cancel them or make life difficult for them. Hateful people have been found in virtually every society throughout human history. Those societies that do best are the ones that minimize the proliferation or creation of hateful people and maximize the quantity of loving, peaceful, creative people.

As I mentioned in the previous chapter, in grade school I was one of very few Black students at predominantly white elementary and middle schools. I encountered a mixture of hateful people and loving, peaceful people. In some cases people reacted negatively to my race, and for others race made no difference at all. I specifically remember one of my classmates by the name of Gerard whose family emigrated from Eastern Europe. They were extremely nice to me, frequently inviting me over for dinner and games. They doubtless had suffered at the hands of individuals who did not particularly care about the rights of others, and I believe that made them more sensitive to the plight of Blacks in America at that time. On the other hand, we frequently had a substitute math teacher who also was from Eastern Europe. She was completely unable to comprehend the fact that I as a Black student consistently achieved the highest scores on the math quizzes. She would write notes to my mother expressing her shock and dismay and would make inappropriate comments in the classroom. Gerard's parents and the math teacher were from the same part of the world but looked at race in very different ways. The point is, racial stereotyping occurs everywhere around the globe and needs to be recognized and combated everywhere.

Another example of unbecoming behavior based on race would occur at the community swimming pool. Again, 99 percent of the population was white, and some were clearly agitated by the fact that we were there. Before being granted access to the pool, everyone had to pass by the lifeguard, who would determine if you were clean enough by rubbing his thumb across your chest to see if any debris was discoverable. For the white kids it was usually only one or two rubs, but for the Black kids they usually rubbed until something appeared, even if it was dead skin. You would then have to reenter the shower and scrub some more. This clearly prejudicial behavior was inspired by the myth that Black people are dirty and that that is partly the reason for their dark skin.

Unfortunately, myths of that nature have frequently accompanied prejudicial behavior against a variety of groups arriving to this nation. There have been myths about Italians, Irish, Germans, Jews, Asians, Africans, Middle Easterners, and others. Obviously, spreading negative rumors about other groups enhances the standing of the group perpetrating the offense. Generally speaking, the more insecure one is with their own value and community standing, the more likely they are to try to denigrate others. Accordingly, the best way to engender nonprejudicial speech and behavior in young people is to build up their self-esteem. When your self-image is good, there is no need to put someone else down.

In the Delray section of Detroit where we lived for a couple of years, there was a community center that was much more integrated, with poor Blacks and poor whites. When team sports were played, the teams were generally broken down along racial lines. Some might think that indicated some form of racism, but it actually reflected the reality that most people choose team members who live near them and associate with them all the time. It's a phenomenon that is similar to the observation of babies preferring familiar-looking faces that was mentioned in the previous chapter.

As with all adolescents, fights frequently broke out, and sometimes they were interracial in nature. When that occurred, the people who gathered around to watch frequently chanted, "A fight, a fight, a [n-word] and a white." Both Black and white observers would join in the chant. You might think that such appalling language would generate animosity, but the same kids would be palling around the next day as if nothing had happened. Although the children observed and acknowledged racial differences, I don't believe they took them nearly as seriously as did the adults. The young people seemed far more interested in having fun than in inflicting physical or emotional pain on others. Unfortunately, many adults in today's American society seem obsessed with promoting their views and suppressing the views of those who disagree with them. This has resulted in the rise of "cancel culture," which is antithetical to the concept of liberty, which is of course one of the foundational cornerstones of our nation.

Cancel culture and Jim Crow racism have much in common. The aim of both is to disenfranchise and control the targeted group. Both cater to our evil angels and ignore the rights of others. Both seek to establish one group of people or opinions as superior to those of the targeted group. Neither should be acceptable in the land of the free. If Americans are manipulated into believing that it is acceptable to harm people or destroy their livelihood simply because there is disagreement between them, the seeds of our national destruction will have been successfully sown.

Even as we witness the destructive nature of cancel

culture and other mechanisms of dividing our society, there is room for optimism. Far more Americans recognize the benefits of living and working together for the good of all than was the case during my adolescence. I remember how excited my brother, Curtis, and I were when we found out that there was a neighborhood football team we might be able to join. We eagerly attended the tryout and the coach was thrilled to have us because we were both extremely fast runners, which would be a tremendous boost for the team. But the problem in the eyes of some of the neighborhood observers was the color of our skin. As we exuberantly headed home that afternoon, we were approached by a group of young white men who told us that we should not return, and if we did, they would drown us in the Detroit River. They appeared to be quite serious, and Curtis and I heeded their warning. We did not tell our mother about the incident, because we did not want to worry her. In this case their racism overrode common sense, which would inform them that the chances of their team being successful would be greatly enhanced by having two people who could outrun everyone else. Hatred, however, is an emotion that is incompatible with logic and common sense.

How many times have people sacrificed potential success in business or other endeavors because they were unwilling to relinquish their prejudices? How much better were the Brooklyn Dodgers when the team accepted Jackie Robinson? If only people could see how utterly ridiculous they are when they base their actions on external appearances and fail to engage those big frontal lobes of the brain that distinguish people from other animals. It is particularly disheartening when one witnesses racist tendencies in young people whose brains are still developing.

I remember when I transitioned from Higgins Elementary School to Wilson Junior High School, both of which were almost exclusively white schools. I was quite excited. I had gone from the dummy in the class to the student receiving the highest grades, and I was beginning to visualize a very successful future in medicine. The journey from home to the school was about a mile and I generally walked. Part of that walk was along the railroad tracks in a relatively secluded area. One day a group of older boys from Wilson Junior High intercepted me on the tracks and told me that I was not allowed to attend their school and that they would kill me if I didn't withdraw. They were carrying sticks with which they hit me to reinforce their threats. Again, I didn't tell my mother about the incident, not wanting to worry her, and I simply changed the route I took to get to school. I remember seeing the leader of that pack of boys in one of my classes a few days later working as the projectionist for a film reel. He saw me and gave me the death stare, but I simply ignored him. That group of boys never sought me out or bothered me again, and I hope that they all matured and found peace, because life is much more peaceful and fulfilling when you don't complicate it by trying to negatively impact the lives of others.

The kinds of encounters that I have described so far are virtually nonexistent these days, demonstrating that significant progress has been made in American society. One would think that perhaps churches with Christian foundations would be more welcoming of racial diversity. When I was in junior high school, we switched our attendance from the Sharon Seventh-day Adventist Church in Inkster, Michigan, to the Melvindale Seventh-day Adventist Church in Melvindale. The former was a Black church and the latter was a white church. The white church was much closer to our home, and my mother, Sonya Carson, had a very thick skin and was not intimidated by the very cool reception in Melvindale. She always had a quick response when members of that church would say something like, "There's a church for colored folks in Inkster that is really nice." Her retort would be, "That's very nice. You should go there and visit." Or sometimes another Black family might be visiting and someone would say to her, "Some colored folks just came in." She would say to them, "Why don't you go and make sure they feel welcome?" After a while the church members stopped making such comments to her, and in fact, many of them began to take a keen interest in Curtis and me due to our stellar academic performance and accumulation of academic awards. We began to socialize with many of the congregation and their families, and by the time I graduated from high school and was heading off to Yale, I had received an abundance of monetary gifts from church members. By that time there was almost never a mention of race to us by church members. I think they saw us as the Carson family and not the Black Carson family. When people get to know each other, minor physical distinctions quickly fade into the background. This is one of the reasons why hard-core racists wanted so much to maintain segregation throughout the entire society.

Ultimately, the vast majority of the church members in Melvindale turned out to be very nice people with whom we got along famously. We would have never known that if we had heeded the advice of many of my mother's friends in the Black churches who told her what a nightmare she would experience if she dared attend a white church. Furthermore, they said it would damage her sons, probably for life. I suspect that at that time a white family attempting to transfer membership to a Black church may have had a similar experience. It was a time of racial immaturity on an evolving scale of racial integration. Now, fifty-plus years later, after making tremendous progress, we are trying to turn back the hands of the clock and make race the central focus of so many lives. We will discuss the reversal of racial progress later in this book.

As I mentioned previously, my early life in Southwest Detroit had been relatively happy. We lived in one of those seven-hundred-square-foot G.I. houses, but it was our house. The yards were tiny, as were the rooms, but after the divorce, as a small child I constantly fantasized about being able to live in that house again. It was a lot better than the tenements that were full of rodents and roaches. My mother worked extremely hard as a domestic, saving every penny until she was able to afford to move us back into that house. I was able to start high school living in the same house that I had started kindergarten in.

Southwestern High School was a basketball powerhouse, but it wasn't much of an academic place of assembly. Nevertheless, I had some terrific teachers who saw a lot of potential in me and went out of their way to help me. There were very few Black teachers at Southwestern even though it was a predominantly Black high school.

Interestingly, the white kids generally stuck together in their little cliques, as did the Black kids and the kids of Middle Eastern descent, of whom there were many. There generally was not a lot of racial tension. That changed markedly when Dr. Martin Luther King Jr. was assassinated. The Black kids rioted, causing great damage, and they were looking for white kids to harm. I, too, was upset about the assassination of Dr. King, but I was also concerned about the safety of the white kids who through no fault of their own were being persecuted. I had a key to the biology lab because I had an after-school job as the lab assistant. I was able to unlock the lab and hide several white students in there until the rioting ended. The peace of the previous summer in Detroit was shattered by the infamous riots that destroyed a significant part of the city. I can still remember the armored vehicles and armed National Guard troops on the streets of my hometown as fires raged and looting prevailed it seemed like everywhere. Detroit, like many other big cities around the country, was a powder keg waiting to explode. Just as unseen, pent-up frustration on behalf of Blacks in the Jim Crow South finally created fertile ground for protests and demonstrations, the subtle but persistent racism in northern cities finally erupted into unimaginable violence and mayhem. To their credit, the administrators and staff at Southwestern High School held conversation sessions with the students over the next few days to help defuse the situation. It is amazing how effective calm conversation can be to restore a rational atmosphere in which harmony can exist. We would do well to remember that in today's America where many factions exist that suppress open conversation and stimulate further division.

Another thing that helped restore a degree of harmony to the streets of Detroit—which looked like a war zone after the 1967 riots—was the success the following year of the Detroit Tigers. The last appearance of the Tigers in the World Series had been in 1945. Not only did they have an exciting season, but they dramatically won the Series in 1968 against the St. Louis Cardinals after being down three games to one. They also had Denny McLain, who won thirty-one games that season, a feat that has not been replicated since that time. There is nothing like a common interest to bring warring factions together. In Detroit, the Tigers were that common interest, whereas in many other cities it might be the football team, the basketball team, a hockey team, or some other entity that brings great pride to the community.

Unfortunately, the team spirit in many places around the country has been injured in recent years because athletes have decided to bring politics into the stadium. Why they feel the necessity to do this is hard to comprehend. When you go to see the doctor or you get on an airplane, you generally are not interested in the doctor's or the pilot's political views. I certainly believe that athletes have every right to believe as they wish, but it's so unnecessary to bring division into what is supposed to be an enjoyable event. It's not as if people who are offended can just leave and easily get a refund. You really have a captive audience, and why would you impose your political views on them rather than allow them to simply enjoy the game?

The unnecessary imposition of our views upon others is an act of self-importance that is not conducive to harmonious coexistence. I saw this frequently in my high school. It took the form of peer pressure, and almost everyone conformed to it. This included the wearing of certain types of clothing and the practice of nontraditional speech. Those who didn't conform were "acting white." By adopting these practices, some of the white kids were fully embraced as "honorary Blacks." One young man in particular by the name of Tommy was known as the "blue-eyed soul brother." He was extremely popular and reveled in his status. Because of my love of classical music and high academic achievement, and my less than fashionable but very neat wardrobe, I was frequently accused of acting white. After such accusations I would simply pose the question "If being smart is acting white, then what is acting Black?" Rarely would someone try to answer that question. No one really wants to do so, because they would obviously be engaging in broad, sweeping generalizations. But isn't that exactly what racists do all the time?

From many of the preceding stories, it is easy to see that race plays a large role in many people's lives. For me it began to diminish in importance as I became a voracious reader. In his book *Up from Slavery*, Booker T. Washington provided compelling reasons not to see oneself as a victim and to create one's own pathway to success. I also read about explorers, inventors, entrepreneurs, doctors, and a host of other people of great accomplishment. It became apparent that color or race had much less to do with success than hard work, vision, and determination. Yes, there were some people who perhaps had a steeper mountain to climb in order to achieve success, but that simply made them stronger and more capable of scaling the next mountain. With that realization, I stopped listening to people who claimed that the system was rigged against the success of Black people. What does in fact increase the chances of failure is a defeatist attitude associated with victimization. This is one of the reasons why those who try to make Blacks feel like long-term victims of a society that once included slavery are doing them no favors and most likely are doing them harm. We need to instill the can-do attitude versus the what-can-you-do-for-me attitude in those people who have been taught that they are victims.

One of my favorite stories in the Bible is about Joseph, who was one of the twelve sons of Jacob. He was sold into slavery by his own brothers, but instead of becoming a victim he said, "I'll be the best slave there ever was." As a result of that attitude, he became the overseer of the captain of the royal guard's household. The captain's wife had eyes for Joseph, but when he rebuffed her advances, she claimed that he had assaulted her, and he ended up in prison. Obviously, the captain did not believe his wife or he would have had Joseph killed, but he needed to protect her honor, such as it was. Again, Joseph refused to be the victim and determined to be the best prisoner there ever was. He obtained an oversight position in the prison and was in place to interpret the dreams of Pharaoh, ending up with a role in government that was second only to Pharaoh himself. That story and the faith it produced in me propelled me through many difficult situations subsequently.

Arriving on the campus of Yale University as a freshman gave me real culture shock. There was real silver in the dining halls and real china. There were lush Oriental rugs and valuable paintings on the mahogany walls. There were abundant fireplaces and all the trappings of wealth and privilege. I had not had a lot of exposure to very rich people and I didn't know how they would react to me. The year was 1969, and it was the first year that Yale admitted women, and also the first year that it admitted a significant number of Black students. I quickly became acquainted with the students and thought that they were all accepting of me. One evening I was preparing to go to dinner with one of my new friends, from Ohio, when I overheard a conversation in the men's room between that individual and another student, who said to him, "Are you actually going to have dinner with that blackie?" Needless to say, I was a bit taken aback, but my friend from Ohio, whose name was Rod, never skipped a beat. He simply responded, "Of course." I never indicated that I had overheard the conversation, but I did realize that for some people in America race was still a factor regardless of their socioeconomic status. That was a hurtful realization, because I had managed to convince myself that the well-heeled intellectual social classes were beyond racial stereotyping and discrimination. Knowing that they were not was an important discovery, since I would be dealing with such individuals for the rest of my life.

During my time at Yale, I also became acquainted with Black students who were quite different from those I had grown up with. One such individual was David, whose father was a professor at a different Ivy League university. David had spent a substantial portion of his youth in Germany and spoke fluent German. He was incredibly smart and often established the high end of the grading curve in our science classes. David enjoyed a very distinguished career in academic medicine and now is the editor of a prestigious medical journal. His excellence in everything made it clear to me that my race should in no way limit my capacity to succeed in whatever field I chose. The kind of excellence that David exhibited was rare for Black students at high-powered universities in those days. It is commonplace today. Those who claim that there has not been much socioeconomic progress among Black people in America obviously are walking around with their eyes closed. I am aware of many Black millionaires, and I have a neighbor in Florida who is a Black billionaire. Only recently has Hollywood begun to depict wealthy, well-heeled Black families in movies. There is still a long way to go to shrink the wealth gap between Black families and white families, but we should acknowledge significant progress.

Another type of Black student that I had not encountered previously was represented by a young man we will call Andy in order to protect his identity. Andy was light-skinned, but no one would have difficulty identifying him as Black. That is, no one except himself. He never spoke to other Black students and strictly associated with white classmates. He even tried to avoid looking at those of us who were Black. I felt sorry for him, because he was obviously engaging in self-loathing behavior rather than enjoying life without the excessive burden of filtering out anything that reminded him of his true ancestry. Believe it or not, there are actually substantial numbers of Black people who are prejudiced against other Black people. They consider themselves superior and can be rather hateful and dismissive of other Black people. One interesting tidbit that few people know is that there were many Black slave owners in the South during the early days of slave trading. Some people don't want to acknowledge that because it contradicts the narrative of innately oppressive white people. The fact of the matter is people are people and human nature is human nature and there are good people and bad people of every racial background.

There is a lot of similarity between the way Blacks and whites act under similar circumstances. But what about some other ethnic groups with backgrounds dissimilar to either of those groups? Let's look at Native Americans, a.k.a. Indians. When the settlers first came to America, they found the Indians to be efficient and cunning hunters and farmers. The early settlers were able to learn a lot from the Indians, but unfortunately the Indians also learned a lot from European settlers. Many of the things they learned were not helpful, such as the use of alcoholic beverages. Subsequently Indians were relocated to reservations. Beginning in the 1980s they were allowed to oversee the development of casinos and assume ownership, as is the case with all other Americans. Those casinos generated enormous wealth for some tribes. Very much like white and Black Americans, some of the tribes were very extravagant, and they lost the drive and search for excellence that used to characterize tribal life. A few years ago, I was contracted to speak at a very large tribal casino because the tribal elders were concerned about the teenagers who benefited significantly from monthly stipends and were not interested in college or other forms of higher education because they already had a very good living derived from casino revenues. The elders were concerned about the future of the tribe if all the young people became dependent upon these very generous subsidies. Their hope was that I could inspire the work ethic once again and show its advantages. I bring that story up to demonstrate that the young people in these Native American nations behaved exactly like their Black and white counterparts. It is human nature to kick back and relax when you have plenty. It was not the race of the young Indians that impeded their educational progress; it was their circumstances.

When I matriculated in medical school at the University of Michigan in 1973, I believed that I had conquered the final hurdle in realizing my dream of becoming a physician. Little did I know, half of the Black students who were admitted did not finish. I soon discovered that there was at least one professor rumored to say that Black people could not pass his course. Admittedly there was very little academic support for those who might not have had a strong background in the sciences, and I saw many of my Black classmates fall by the wayside. Was this racism, ambivalence, or apathy on behalf of the administration of the medical school? I myself was counseled by my faculty advisor to either drop out of medical school or take a substantially reduced load following a very poor performance on the first set of comprehensive examinations. Fortunately, after I sought wisdom from God, my self-analysis yielded the fact that I learned very little from lectures but retained a great deal from reading. I began skipping the lectures and spending that time reading, which resulted in dramatic academic improvement.

Interestingly, in the medical school class that graduated a year before mine, the number one graduate in the class was a Black female who went on to become a pediatric neurosurgeon. In the class that graduated a year after mine, the number one graduate was a Black male who is now the chief of neurosurgery at a well-known medical center in California. The point is, not all of the Black students were struggling academically. It is incumbent upon institutions of higher learning to analyze academic shortfalls and remedy them rather than allow people who clearly have intellectual talent to fail, and then to claim, as some less charitable people do, that this is evidence of intellectual inferiority. Fortunately, the University of Michigan and a number of medical schools now recognize that different people learn in different ways and have found a variety of teaching methods to accommodate those differences.

As you can see from reading this chapter, race definitely played a role in my psychosocial development. It resulted in the alteration of some of my plans, such as in the case of the neighborhood football league. Obviously, later there were much bigger alterations in my plans. One of the questions is, is it possible for us to have a society that minimizes rather than maximizes the differences between people of different races? We all have the same kind of brain and similar needs and desires. We tend to act the same way in certain circumstances, and we laugh and cry for the same reasons. As we explore many deep issues surrounding race, let us remember that celebrating our diversity is a good thing as long as we don't permit that celebration to morph into a hierarchical system that values one group over another.

CHAPTER 3

The History of Slavery and Racism in America

Slavery in the World

You may have heard it said that slavery has been around since people have been around. And that would not be far off the mark. Before there were strategic alliances and governmental allies, there were ancient tribal civilizations. From time to time they would go to war for various reasons, one of which was to expand their kingdoms. In many cases the victors of these tribal wars would enslave any survivors who remained after the dust settled, including orphans. Some historians even claim that every society at some time in its history has experienced slavery.[1]

Also, within some societies there were those who settled their debts by becoming indentured slaves, working off what they owed for a prescribed number of years.

In the early 1900s the discovery of a diorite stone stele (pillar) covered with inscriptions gave the world new insight into the culture of one of these ancient civilizations. Found in an area where history showed a warring country had existed, and most likely those warriors had brought it there as a part of their spoils, it traveled again to France, where it was deciphered and translated in only one year. At that time it revealed the "earliest example of a written legal code."[2]

The code of 282 laws inscribed on the stele included rules about slaves and gave an early example of the notions "an eye for an eye" and "innocent until proven guilty." So slavery existed more than seventeen hundred years prior to Christ's birth. This code had been literally set in stone by the Babylonian king Hammurabi, who ruled Mesopotamia (the area currently known as Iraq) from 1792 to 1750 BC. Its influence on modern history is evidenced in many ways, including in our own United States, for on the wall near the ceiling of the Supreme Court, King Hammurabi is carved in bas-relief as one of the contributors to our current law.

One of the earliest accounts of the African slave trade is cited by Davidson College professor Michael Guasco, the author of *Slaves and Englishmen: Human Bondage in the Early Modern Atlantic World*. "The first example we have of Africans being taken against their will and put on board European ships would take the story back to 1441," writes Guasco, referring to when the Portuguese took twelve natives they captured in north Africa back to Portugal to serve as slaves.³

As it was in ancient civilizations, tribes in Africa also would enslave survivors of their battles. Some less scrupulous individuals on the African continent discovered the economic value of selling their enemies and worked with slave traders to gain financial profit.

Slavery in the Americas

Although many history books claim that the first slaves to arrive in America landed in 1619 in Jamestown, the first permanent English settlement, several temporary settlements occurred prior to then by colonists from England and other countries.

Consider Christopher Columbus. Around fifty years after the Portuguese transported slaves from Africa to Europe, Columbus made his way across the Atlantic, seeking a shorter route to India to obtain treasures such as gold and exotic spices for Spain. When Columbus arrived in the islands of the New World in 1492, he found the indigenous people to be extremely friendly and docile. He wrote that they "are so naïve...they offer to share with anyone."⁴ These friendly natives were quite hale, hearty, and handsome but were not familiar with the guns and swords of their visitors. The weapons they used were spears made of cane.

Columbus imagined huge potential gains as he considered using the natives to work in mines for gold and on plantations. His comments in his report to the king and queen reflect his somewhat opportunistic bent. And I suppose if one is seeking ways to make a profit and discover treasures that would expand the coffers of the crown, it would seem logical to attempt to take advantage of the natives' naïveté. His actual words were "They would make fine servants...with fifty men we could subjugate them all and make them do whatever we want."[5]

On his return trip to Spain in the spring of 1493, a portion of Columbus's cargo was the gold they sought, but the hold of his ship also contained hundreds of natives of the Caribbean islands, although only about two-fifths of the captives survived the extremely rough conditions of the voyage. But morality was not a consideration here, just as it wasn't with the natives from the African continent, even though Columbus mentioned God in his report, saying, "Let us in the name of the Holy Trinity go on sending all the slaves that can be sold."[6]

It was estimated that the island where he established the first European settlement in the Americas, Hispaniola (where Haiti and the Dominican Republic are located), was inhabited by over half a million people when Columbus first arrived. But the population decreased to twenty-nine thousand in less than twenty-five years. There were hardly any people left at all by 1550. This attrition was due primarily to the harsh conditions of slavery, and the catastrophic spread of diseases brought by the Europeans to which the natives had no immunity. These facts didn't stop the expansion of slavery to other Caribbean isles.

One of the Spanish settlers to arrive in the Caribbean was Bartolomé de Las Casas, in 1502. While in the islands, he studied to become a priest and became a vehement voice against the cruelty toward the natives of the Caribbean, continuously speaking out about their inhumane treatment. In his writings, he said the Spaniards were "not just cruel, but extraordinarily cruel so that harsh and bitter treatment would prevent Indians from daring to think of themselves as human beings or having a minute to think at all." It may have been in a moment of intense frustration to lessen the severe suffering he witnessed daily that he suggested to the Spaniards (but later regretted) that slaves be brought from Africa. And it wasn't long afterward that exactly that occurred. (This was prior to Las Casas's death in 1566.)

However, after Las Casas spoke before Spain's parliament in 1519, King Charles actually granted funding to establish settlements with free Indians and Spaniards working together.[7] The experiment didn't last long, but the next time Las Casas spoke before parliament, the Leyes Nuevas (New Laws) were passed, limiting the length of Indian servitude to one generation.[8]

In the 1500s, African slaves arrived on the Florida coast in Spanish ships. "There were significant numbers who were brought in as early as 1526," says Boston University professor Linda Heywood, coauthor of *Central Africans, Atlantic Creoles, and the Foundation of the Americas, 1585–1660*.[9] When the Spanish tried that year to found a colony in what is now South Carolina, bringing along some of these slaves, the captives rebelled, stymieing the attempt. So not all slaves were docile, and as you've probably already concluded, establishing settlements was not an easy job, particularly with so many unknowns: food sources, weather challenges, competition for survival from native animals and peoples as well as from other nations.

British involvement can be found as early as the late 1500s, when Sir Francis Drake, a known slave trader, sailed to the shores of what is now the Outer Banks of North Carolina more than once. It has been surmised by some historians that he may have had slaves on board to help with the work.

In another occurrence of note, John White, who had come as an artist to capture the surroundings in paintings to share with the crown, was forced to return to England for supplies after a couple of years, leaving behind his granddaughter, the first child of English descent to be born in the New World. When he returned about two years later, all the people who had been left in the settlement had disappeared.[10]

St. Augustine, Florida, the Longest-Surviving Colony

In 1565, a few years before Jamestown's establishment in 1619, and only a few hundred miles down the coast, when Spanish conquistador Pedro Menéndez de Avilés stepped on the shores of La Florida, there were Black slaves with him as well as Black crew members, all there to establish the settlement of St. Augustine. (La Florida, the land claimed by Ponce de Leon in 1513 for Spain, extended north through what is now Georgia and into South Carolina.) According to historians, St. Augustine is the "oldest continuously occupied European settlement in North America...but the settlement was plagued by a myriad of problems from indigenous rebellions to pirate attacks, most famously that of Sir Francis Drake in 1586."[11]

But they rebuilt. St. Augustine was recognized by the ship captains as a strategic location to protect treasure ships, and it became heavily supported by the Spanish crown once the royals were convinced. The Catholic Church was also a big supporter, as it could envision

St. Augustine as a unique opportunity to convert natives and slaves. The town remained the center of the Spanish colonial slave trade from the 1500s (before Jamestown) into the early 1800s.[12]

South and North

Actually, slavery was not limited to the American South. There were also slaves in the northern colonies. The institution was not as widespread there, however, as farming was not as big a part of the economic engine up north, and industries were more diversified.

But in the South the large labor force was critical to the very survival of the economy. It simply took a lot of workers to manage the many acres of crops. From another perspective, abolishing slavery would give the northern companies a competitive economic edge over their southern counterparts. The cost of workers for the South would be an economic handicap with their labor-intensive cotton and tobacco crop production. Even with white European indentured labor, it would still be quite a challenge, because labor would now cost the owners, and even if the costs were low, they would be multiplied by tens or hundreds. Another concern would be about perpetuating helpers. Since the children of indentured servants would belong to their parents and not automatically to the masters/owners as the African slaves' offspring would, the planters would lose that benefit as well.[13]

Treatment

As an example of the tenor of the times, in 1705 a law was enacted in Virginia that directed how different types of slaves were to be treated. Christian slaves (their euphemism for "white") would only serve until age twenty-four, while non-Christian (nonwhite) slaves would never be released from bondage, even if they became Christian:

> Be it enacted, by the governor, council, and burgesses..., That all servants brought into this country without indenture, if the said servants be *christians* [i.e., white] and of christian parentage, and above nineteen years of age, 'till they shall become twenty-four years of age, and no longer.[14] (emphasis added)

The same document contained this verbiage concerning non-Christians:

> And also be it enacted, by the authority aforesaid..., That all servants imported and brought into this country, by sea or land, who were *not christians* in their native country...*shall be accounted and be slaves*, and such be here bought and sold notwithstanding a conversion to christianity afterward. (emphasis added)

So it is clear that slaves of different ethnicities were to be treated quite differently. It was also somewhat surprising to discover that in the colonies, Native Americans and those of African descent could at one time own slaves. This fact is supported by laws that were enacted to restrict ownership of ethnically different slaves. The law below was passed in the Virginia House of Burgesses that those of African descent as well as Native Americans could not own Christian (white) slaves:

> And for a further christian care and usage of all christian servants, Be it also enacted, by the authority aforesaid, and it is hereby enacted, That *no negros, mulattos, or Indians, although christians, or Jews, Moors, Mahometans, or other infidels, shall, at any time, purchase any christian servant, nor any other, except of their own complexion, or such as are declared slaves by this act.* (emphasis added)

Western World Trend

However, historians also have commented on the global reach that slavery had and how English, Spanish, Portuguese, and other slave traders were all collectively involved in and responsible for perpetuating this blight on humanity. "We would do well to remember that much of what played out in places like Virginia were the result of things that had already happened in Mexico, Central America, the Caribbean, Peru, Brazil and elsewhere," says Guasco, the Davidson College professor.[15]

It was the common practice of the times. And each probably justified their involvement by saying, "Well, everyone else is doing it." But just because others are doing something doesn't make it right.

The American Civil War

After so many countries had experienced the horrors of slavery at some point or another, you would think that by the nineteenth century, eighteen hundred years after Christ, maybe some would have awakened and stopped it.

Well, not many years after that turn of the century, abolitionists in the United States decided to take their faith seriously and work toward abolishing slavery. And southerners, considering the impact on their comfortable way of life and a series of events, were becoming alarmed about their livelihoods being threatened. Although the Kansas-Nebraska Act of 1854 made a way for slavery to expand westward as the country expanded, several bloody encounters between pro- and anti-slavery settlers in Kansas occurred over the next five years, and a new Republican political party was established to remove slavery from the culture. The *Dred Scott* decision supported slavery, but the raid at Harpers Ferry by John Brown did the opposite.

And when President Abraham Lincoln was elected (and it was known that he was a northern sympathizer), seven southern states decided to take action and secede.

1861: Contrabands of War

On May 23, 1861, three male slaves crossed the James River, escaping to Fort Monroe, Virginia, a federal installation. They were seeking a place of refuge. The situation took the commanding officer of the fort, Union major general Benjamin F. Butler, by surprise, as he had never had to deal with runaway slaves prior to this. (And this was at the time the state of Virginia was seceding from the Union shortly after the war started.)

Not very long after the men arrived, a major from a nearby Virginia state militia came to the fort, claiming that the runaways belonged to his commanding officer. General Butler, thinking quickly, responded thusly: "But you say you have seceded, so you cannot consistently claim them. I shall hold these negroes as contraband of war, since they are...claimed as your property."[16]

Contraband of war is defined as "a term in international law that refers to a belligerent's right to prevent an enemy from receiving goods of value in waging war and to seize and condemn any cargo shipped by a neutral nation to a warring power, usually on the high seas."[17]

Slaves gained new status with the new term bestowing value upon them, certainly not as demeaning as so many words that had previously been used to describe them. The term caught on, bringing new hope to those who had been and still were under the burden of slavery.

The Haven Called the Freedmen's Colony

In February 1862, less than a year into the war, the Union's victory on Roanoke Island made a huge difference in the fight for freedom.[18] The island is located on the Outer Banks of North Carolina, and after Union soldiers conquered the Confederate stronghold, they freed the slaves there and established a safe destination for other slaves to go. Many slaves were able to escape their plights and become free at this haven of refuge. Some freedmen joined the military, and others helped in various trades. Freed women helped as well with domestic services.[19]

Emancipation

As the new president, Lincoln's main goal from the beginning of the war was to reunite the country, and he was willing to do whatever it took to achieve it. However, he had to be convinced that slavery needed to be abolished in order to accomplish that goal. This was shown in one of his statements to the press:

> If I could save the Union without freeing any slave, I would do it; and if I could save it by freeing all the slaves, I would do it; and if I could save it by freeing some and leaving others alone, I would also do that.[20]

As Union armies penetrated deeper into the South, slaves fled in droves as they saw their way to freedom. While Lincoln considered this and the concept of contrabands of war, he became convinced. The president's Emancipation Proclamation took effect in 1863 in the states that had seceded.

Juneteenth

In April 1865, General Robert E. Lee of the Confederacy surrendered to General Ulysses S. Grant of the Union army in the parlor of Wilmer McLean in the village called Appomattox Court House. The war was over. No more bloodshed.[21]

However, it took time for everyone to hear about it. Although the commercial telegraph had been invented in 1837, Samuel Morse's company didn't complete the lines from Washington, DC, to New York until 1846, and there were some areas that still weren't "in the loop" in 1865.

On June 19, 1865, Union troops led by U.S. general Gordon Granger rode into Galveston, Texas, to deliver the news that the war was over and all slaves were free, reading "General Orders No. 3" out loud to the people assembled there:

> The people of Texas are informed that, in accordance with a proclamation from the Executive of the United States, all slaves are free.

It had been two months since General Lee's surrender over two and a half years since the Emancipation Proclamation had been delivered. These were the last people to hear the news. But now every person knew and could join in the celebration.

Juneteenth was initially celebrated on its first anniversary in 1866 in Texas. It wasn't long before other states celebrated as well.[22] In 2021, Juneteenth National Independence Day became the eleventh federal holiday to be recognized nationwide by the U.S. government.[23]

Reconstruction

Can you imagine the difficulty people would have in trying to reconstruct a whole culture? New laws were in place, but the people who were to live and abide by these laws had been living in a totally different manner for several generations.

From the freed slaves' point of view, they had finally obtained what they had been hoping and praying for since the 1600s. Their way of life had changed dramatically for the better. They no longer had to always look down and be submissive but could with dignity look other people in the eye. They no longer had to respond to the dictates of others no matter how difficult or inconvenient or painful those might be. They no longer had to try to avoid the master's temper and lashings with a whip or other terrible punishments. They no longer had to take on any mistreatment that could be bestowed upon them without any concern. They could live as families and not have to leave loved ones behind when sold to another slave owner. They could actually live as everyone else's equal.

As for the slave owners, they had lost their livelihoods, or at least suffered great losses of income due to the reduction in the number of affordable workers. Their way of life had changed dramatically as well, but for the worse. They no longer had the comfort of what was familiar. They no longer had people to work for them. They could no longer delegate tasks and get other work done while menial tasks were carried out by slave helpers. They no longer had people to boss around to do jobs they didn't want to do. They no longer had servants at their beck and call. They could no longer take out their frustrations on a subservient being who happened to be handy. They now had to take care of everything themselves or hire someone else to do it. With their reduced finances, it wasn't feasible to hire cooks and maids to clean and babysitters and enough farmhands to keep production at a level consistent with what they were accustomed to.

With the Thirteenth Amendment's abolition of slavery, the government was faced with trying to peacefully integrate these two factions in seven states after an extremely bloody war that had touched every family with some sort of grief. This period that lasted from 1865 to 1877 was known as Reconstruction. There were four million new citizens who needed to be assimilated into a new culture. And the new president, Andrew Johnson, was a southern sympathizer.

So it's not surprising that in 1865–66, under the administration of President Johnson, new southern state legislatures "passed restrictive 'Black Codes' to control the labor and behavior of former enslaved people and other African Americans."[24]

Of course, the North didn't appreciate this, and the pendulum swung back the other way. A more radical Republican Party philosophy evolved and manifested itself in the 1867 Reconstruction Act, in which Americans of color were given a voice in government and served in state legislatures as well as the federal one. And southern states were required to ratify the Fourteenth and Fifteenth Amendments granting citizenship, constitutional protection, and the right to vote to previously enslaved people.

It's not difficult to imagine the whiplash reaction from southern states yielding the Ku Klux Klan, whose violent practices returned the South to their previous state of believed supremacy through supreme intimidation. And state and local governments pushed back with Jim Crow laws that made racial segregation legal.

Prosperous Black Communities

Tired of living in fear, many freed slaves were drawn to the idea of living in homogeneous towns across the country, where everyone would be of the same race. The Homestead Act (1862) was a great federal tool used to populate western territories with the lure of inexpensive land. And freed slaves particularly appreciated the opportunity to own land, since that was fairly impossible to obtain in the South.

Between eighty and two hundred towns were established, with promises of land appreciation as other developments, such as railways, would arrive. Many towns did very well, establishing their own schools, churches, and businesses and enjoying self-government. But most disappeared within a few years when the promised developments did not arrive.[25]

Segregation

In the midst of Jim Crow, African American Homer Plessy claimed that his constitutional rights were being violated when he wasn't allowed to travel in a train car reserved for whites. The Supreme Court ruling in the *Plessy v. Ferguson* case of 1896 upheld the constitutionality of racial segregation under the "separate but equal" doctrine.

The idea of "separate but equal" was simply another way

to prevent equality, because facilities for whites were always better-designed, better-built, and better-supplied than those for Americans of color. For example, in a white school every student would be provided with a textbook in a particular subject. In a Black school, students would have to share books because there would not be enough to go around.

Segregation was not limited to schools. Anything public was subject to it: public transportation like buses and trains, public bathrooms, public drinking fountains, zoos, libraries, fairs, park benches, playgrounds, hospitals, even areas of stores. In several states white and Black students were required to receive separate textbooks. This way of thinking was even practiced in courts, where different Bibles were used for white people and Black people to swear on.

Segregation even extended to sexuality. "New Orleans mandated the segregation of prostitutes according to race... Marriage and cohabitation between white and Black people was strictly forbidden in most Southern states."[26]

The Civil Rights Movement

The problem wasn't only inequalities in schools and other public facilities, but also in opportunities. Americans of color were not considered equal and were discriminated against with respect to job opportunities and housing, banking services, voting, and other things that really matter.

In 1957, a humble preacher in Montgomery, Alabama,

by the name of Dr. Martin Luther King Jr. founded the Southern Christian Leadership Conference along with Ralph Abernathy, Bayard Rustin, and Fred Shuttlesworth. (On a side note, my wife Candy's maiden name is Rustin, and although she never met him in person, Bayard Rustin was her dad's cousin.) This was a group of African American pastors, businessmen, and other pillars of the community who were interested in changing the inequalities that existed in spite of the legitimate legal structures that were in place. In seminary, the biblical principles to "love your neighbors and pray for your persecutors" synced in MLK's mind with Ghandi's nonviolence as a good method to effect change. And so the protests and marches began.

In cities where King and his followers protested, they were met with gushing water from fire hoses, strong enough to knock a person down. Sometimes snarling dogs were released on the protestors by the police. And sometimes they were taken to jail.

Meetings to strategize on desegregation and reduction of inequalities were often held at a local hotel owned by A. G. Gaston. (We had a chance to have lunch with him a few years before he died.) This entrepreneur extraordinaire was a self-made African American millionaire who would make his mark in spite of living in an extremely racist environment. He owned a bank as well as the only quality hotel in the city that would admit people of color. He had other businesses as well and used much of his profits to help fund the civil rights movement.

When the landmark court case *Brown v. Board of Education* was settled by the Supreme Court in 1954, the justices unanimously ruled that segregation was not in compliance with the Constitution. But progress was slow, as states felt the decision from the Supreme Court violated their right to manage their educational systems. In 1959 over 90 percent of African American students were still attending segregated schools.[27]

The Southern Christian Leadership Conference teamed up with other civil rights groups, including the Alabama Christian Movement for Human Rights (ACMHR), which was founded by Fred Shuttlesworth to make Birmingham an example for the rest of the country to follow. King and Shuttlesworth "conceived of a protest campaign to work toward the desegregation of the city. The campaign, known as the Birmingham Campaign or Project C—C for confrontation—consisted of a four-part strategy including small-scale sit-ins, a generalized boycott of the downtown business district, mass marches, and finally a call on outsiders to descend on Birmingham."[28] In addition to providing voter registration and leadership training, the SCLC "played a major part in the civil rights march on Washington, D.C., in 1963 and in notable antidiscrimination and voter-registration efforts in Albany, Georgia, and Birmingham and Selma, Alabama, in the early 1960s—campaigns that spurred passage of the federal Civil Rights Act of 1964 and the Voting Rights Act of 1965."[29]

Working Toward Equality

In 1961, after serving nine years in the Air Force, James Meredith applied to the University of Mississippi, an all-white school, and was accepted. However, when the university officials discovered that he was African American, they rescinded the acceptance. With help from the National Association for the Advancement of Colored People (NAACP), Meredith filed a discrimination lawsuit. (Segregation was no longer legal after the *Brown v. Board of Education* ruling in 1954.) Although the state courts ruled against Meredith, the case landed in the Supreme Court, which ruled in his favor.

However, though the legalities were in order, the mindset of those connected with the institution of higher learning fondly nicknamed "Ole Miss" was worlds apart from the Supreme Court ruling. History.com says of Meredith, "When he tried to register on September 20, 1962, he found the entrance to the office blocked by Mississippi Governor Ross Barnett. On September 28, the governor was found guilty of civil contempt and was ordered to cease his interference with desegregation at the university or face arrest and a fine of $10,000 a day. Two days later, Meredith was escorted onto the Ole Miss campus by U.S. Marshals, setting off riots that resulted in the deaths of two students."[30]

When the riots broke out, according to Biography.com, "Attorney General Robert Kennedy sent 500 U.S. Marshals to the scene. Additionally, President John F. Kennedy sent military police, troops from the Mississippi National Guard and officials from the U.S. Border Patrol to keep the peace. On October 1, 1962, Meredith became the first Black student to enroll."[31]

In 1963, another historically significant event took place when Meredith became the first Ole Miss graduate of color. His degree was in political science.

The March Against Fear

In early June 1966, civic-minded James Meredith determinedly began a 220-mile solo walk from Memphis, Tennessee, to Jackson, Mississippi. This "March Against Fear" was to encourage Blacks to register to vote and was also in protest of the inequalities still extant in his home state of Mississippi. Suddenly, on June 6, he was wounded by a sniper's bullet and ended up in the hospital. However, three civil rights leaders came to "lift up his torch" and continue the courageous March Against Fear on his behalf. They were Dr. Martin Luther King Jr., president of the Southern Christian Leadership Conference; Stokely Carmichael, leader of the Student Nonviolent Coordinating Committee; and Floyd McKissick, leader of the Congress of Racial Equality (CORE). Meredith actually recovered quickly enough that he was able to join the other three near the end of the journey, and the fearless four, along with around 15,000 sympathizers, arrived in Jackson on June 26.[32]

Together, It Can Be Done

There have been so many who have been willing to work toward that seemingly elusive goal of "equality, and freedom and justice for all." They did not always agree on the methods to achieve it, as you've seen with the nonviolent protests led by Dr. King as contrasted with the Black Power movement's promotion of a strong self-image and self-sufficiency.

Some groups were multipurpose, such as the Black Panther Party for Self-Defense (that group's original name), which was considered militant but carried guns legally and conducted armed citizen patrols in large cities like Oakland. The Black Panthers also provided social programs like free breakfast for children and free health care in at least thirteen Black American communities.

But keeping the issues at the forefront of the news and keeping people informed and aware was a good start. Knowledge is power. Once knowledge has been disseminated, you can reason together.

Attitudes: Then and Now

A few years ago, when Candy was in middle school (she would say, "Don't laugh," because she knows it was more than a few, "but it sounds better than saying the actual number!"), she had a music teacher who was, shall we say, a little quirky. He was fine most of the time. But one day he asked her a question that she couldn't answer. He wanted her to pronounce words that she hadn't seen before that were in a songbook. The reason she couldn't pronounce them was because they were written in a slave dialect (she found this out later). And she had no clue how to say them, even though she had learned some French and Spanish by then. (Later on she just figured that this forty-something white male teacher had mistakenly assumed that since her skin was darker than his that she would have knowledge of slave dialects ingrained in her somehow.)

Well, Candy's home situation was somewhat unique. Her mom was a teacher who demanded correct English grammar *all the time*. Her mom's parents were even more unique: Her grandfather was a physician and her grandmother was a nurse (certainly a rarity in the 1920s), so Candy's mom had probably never seen anything like this either. And being a "tween" then, Candy admits, she was afraid to try to sound the words out because the other kids would probably laugh at her.

The teacher persisted for about five minutes of valuable class time before he finally gave up and sent Candy to the principal's office for not being cooperative. Keep in mind, she *never* went to the principal's office, except to take them homemade goodies every once in a while on special days. (Teachers' kids are encouraged to do that, you know.)

Anyway, Candy waited and waited in the hot seat in the principal's office. She got a few strange stares as visitors wondered why she was there. However, she wasn't too concerned, since she knew she hadn't done anything wrong.

But, boy, was Candy ready to see the principal when she finally got there! All the apprehension that had been building up in spite of her innocence fled as she anticipated finally getting out of the hot seat.

The principal calmly sat down in her office chair and pointed to the chair in front of her desk for Candy to sit. When she asked Candy to explain why she had been sent to her office, Candy tried to answer as politely and thoroughly and in as few words as possible.

The principal's response? She apologized for the teacher! She said that she had received complaints about him for some time and that he would be going to another school next year!

In a way Candy kind of felt sorry for him. He had some misconstrued preconceived notion that anybody with brown skin would be born with slave language in their mouth. Strange ideas born of ignorance. As a teacher, he should have understood that each person has unique life experiences and is not necessarily the same as others with the same skin color. In America, we value each individual as a unique being and as someone who can bring a special perspective to the table, so we can work together to come up with commonsense solutions to problems.

That was back in the 1960s. Now, several decades later, I believe that we've progressed to a point where people are more open-minded about each other and believe that people are indeed created equal.

Back then, there were very few Black-owned businesses, very few Black quarterbacks, very few Emmy Award winners who were Black. But you can go online now and find many articles about successful Black businessmen and businesswomen, record-breaking numbers of Black quarterbacks in the NFL, and Black actors and actresses who have won awards.

Real progress has been made. But there are those who want you to believe that things are worse rather than better than decades ago. And it's just not true. These people have their own narratives that they are trying to impose upon our society. But this is not the American way.

America was founded on cornerstone principles of faith, liberty, community, and life. And many of our predecessors were willing to suffer and give their lives to perpetuate those cornerstones for us to enjoy. We should do no less to ensure that future generations will have at least the same opportunities and privileges that we've come to know and appreciate.

CHAPTER 4

Guilt and Victimhood Surrounding Race

IN RECENT YEARS, WE HAVE HEARD a lot of conversations about white guilt. This is particularly prevalent on university campuses and in environments that are "woke." Supposedly, white people who feel guilt and remorse because of the plight of racial minorities are socially sensitive and therefore are morally superior to whites who do not feel that guilt. They have become defensive about the whole concept of white privilege, which goes hand in hand with white guilt.

One way to understand white guilt is to look at it through the eyes of a disadvantaged racial minority. Many Black men who are carefully scrutinized when they go into the corner drugstore might say that white privilege is displayed when a white man of similar age and apparel would likely not receive that degree of scrutiny. There are multiple other situations where white people seem to get the benefit of the doubt and Black people do not.

I very specifically remember a situation in the early 2000s when I was trying to get to a volunteer fire station in rural Maryland to vote. The polling station closed at eight o'clock, but if you were in line before that time, you could vote. I had finished all of my operative cases that day, made rounds, and expeditiously made my way to the polling place and was in line ten minutes before closing. People were still voting and I was very pleased with myself for having gotten there in time. I was the last person in line and the only Black person in the fire station. One of the voting officials came to me and said that voting was over and that I would not be allowed to cast my vote. I explained to her that I had arrived at 7:50 p.m., which was ten minutes before the termination of voting. She callously walked away and said voting was over. This woman had no idea who I was or how I would vote, but in my opinion, she made assumptions about how I would vote based on my color. If I had been white and someone she perceived to be aligned with her politically, I suspect she would have permitted my vote. That is what I mean by white privilege. The kinds of thoughts I had that evening generally are not entertained by those who are privileged in our society.

I cannot prove that the voting incident was a case of racial bias, but it is hard to explain it in any other way.

When you don't even have to worry about racial bias, you are in a privileged position. Instead of recognizing that these types of incidents are rapidly declining in American society, some have chosen to highlight and magnify them in order to bring them to a level of awareness that prevents them from occurring. Unfortunately, they want not only the woman who was officiating to feel guilty, but all the bystanders who did or said nothing as well. By taking every incident of perceived racial discrimination and magnifying it and repeating it incessantly, the case for systemic racism is made. If we took every case of people being bitten by dogs and magnified it and repeated it incessantly, in a relatively short time there would be serious conversations about removing dogs from our society (even though a careful and fair analysis of the data coupled with objective conversations would lead to a different conclusion).

Guilt in general often causes people to do things that they might not ordinarily do in order to assuage their internal discomfort. Some people are particularly adept at causing others to feel guilty and use this as a form of manipulation. This manipulation can occur with individuals or on a much larger scale to impact social policies.

I was a psychology major in college, and at that time my intention was to become a psychiatrist. One of the courses I took was about commercial marketing. Professional marketers have been manipulating people with guilt and shame for a very long time. Sometimes their manipulation can be socially useful, as was the case with the effort to get people to stop smoking because the secondhand smoke was harming innocent bystanders. The political class and big tech have also become quite skilled at using guilt and shame to manipulate public opinion. When it comes to social engineering, there are few tools as effective as these two entities. By convincing large numbers of white Americans that they are responsible for the plight of minorities, irrational public policies such as "defund the police" can be propagated.

Another tool for manipulating public opinion and subsequently public policy is Black and minority victimization. As a child and adolescent, I vividly remember the prevalence of conversations about evil white people and how they were keeping Black people down. Were there some white people who were doing that? Absolutely! But my mother adamantly refused to accept that reality as an excuse for failure. She readily acknowledged the existence of racism but refused to accept it as the principal reason for failure. Instead, she constantly recited a poem called "Yourself to Blame" by Mayme White Miller. It goes as follows:

> *If things go bad for you,*
> *And make you a bit ashamed,*
> *Often you will find out that*
> *You have yourself to blame*

Swiftly we ran to mischief
And then the bad luck came
Why do we fault others
We have ourselves to blame

Whatever happens to us,
Here are the words we say,
"Had it not been for so and so,
Things wouldn't have gone that way"

And if you are short of friends,
I'll tell you what to do
Make an examination,
You'll find the fault's in you

You're the captain of your ship,
So agree with the same
If you travel downward,
You have yourself to blame

Now, can't you just hear the chorus? "He's blaming the victims. How cruel and insensitive." What actually is cruel is convincing people that they are victims and do not have control of their own destiny. If you believe you are a victim, you are a victim. One of the things that quickly made America into a great nation was its "can do" attitude. This means that no matter how great the obstacles appeared to be, one would find a way around them. This is a theme that I heard constantly from my mother, who absolutely was determined to make sure that my brother, Curtis, and I did not adopt the victim mentality.

The "woke" left denies the existence of American exceptionalism, but in fact it was that can-do attitude that rapidly propelled us from a group of ragtag militiamen to the pinnacle of the world. Victimhood, on the other hand, allows one to blame others for their shortfalls or even for their legitimate problems. If it's someone else's fault, then you don't have to do anything yourself to rectify the situation. It is human nature to want to blame someone else for our problems. Creationists can harken back to the story of Adam and Eve in the Bible. When it was discovered that the couple had violated the command not to eat of the fruit from the tree of the knowledge of good and evil, Adam blamed his wife for giving him the fruit, and she in turn blamed the serpent, who felt that God was unfair. On the other hand, evolutionists blame the environment for all changes both good and bad.

As long as Black Americans see white Americans as their oppressors, it lessens their responsibility to solve their own problems. For instance, Black-on-Black crime is at epidemic levels in many of our large cities that have Black leadership. Nevertheless, if the argument can be made that the system is systemically racist, then one can say it doesn't matter whether the mayor and other leaders are Black or not because the racial disadvantages are baked into the system. Attempts are also made to convince Latinos, Native Americans, and others that the American system is biased against them and they are unlikely to get a fair break. This has had a devastating effect on the Native American population, in which poverty and underachievement run rampant. Alcoholism and drug abuse, particularly with methamphetamines, remain at epidemic levels despite government programs and attempts by many philanthropic organizations to ameliorate the problem.

Some minority groups have not succumbed to the temptation of victimhood. The Vietnamese refugees are a prime example. It was not unusual for multiple Vietnamese families to live together, combining their resources and helping those left behind as they emerged from poverty. It was truly amazing how quickly they would go from sweeping the grounds or pumping gas at a 7-Eleven to owning the franchise.

When slavery officially ended in America, many Black families were very industrious and formed their own independent communities with great success. There was a lot of emphasis on education, family, and God. Probably the most famous of these communities was the Greenwood district of Tulsa, Oklahoma. Prosperity had grown to the point that the area was referred to as the "Black Wall Street." Bogus claims of an assault on a white woman by a Black man led to the wanton destruction of the Greenwood community, including aerial assaults. As with many of the race riots in the late nineteenth and early twentieth centuries, there was a lot of jealousy and a feeling of entitlement among white communities, to the extent that with the slightest provocation they would seize upon the opportunity to destroy Black wealth and progress. As these various incidents are coming to light recently, white guilt has exponentially increased and is being encouraged by things like critical race theory.

There certainly are reasons that many white people might feel guilty about some of the atrocities of the past. Just to demonstrate how much things have changed, look at the story of Jack Johnson, who was the heavyweight boxing champion of the world in the early 1900s. There were many calls by Americans for a white champion to defeat him, even though he was a patriotic red-blooded American himself. The problem was the color of his skin. That precluded support for him from a large number of racist fellow citizens. On July 4, 1910, a championship match was held between Johnson and the famous "Great White Hope" by the name of James Jeffries. Twenty-two thousand white people attended the match, which was heavily publicized and promoted as the fight of the century that would reestablish white supremacy in the ring. When Johnson knocked out Jeffries in the fifteenth round, the white world was stunned. The anger was palpable and there were race riots in fifty cities, with twenty people being killed. That kind of racial bias would be unthinkable today, but it was commonplace in America in the not-too-distant past.

In the early days of America, it was discovered that

Europeans were very fond of tobacco products, which could be readily produced without excessive expense by using enslaved labor in the New World. That was the beginning of the discovery of the incredible economic value that could be gained by exploiting slaves. Initially many of the slaves were poor or orphaned whites along with Blacks and even Indians. The Black slaves were able to endure harsh conditions better than any of the other types, and therefore America moved rapidly in a direction of importing massive numbers of enslaved Africans. It is difficult to estimate the economic value that America realized from enslaved labor. This is the reason that there have been so many calls for reparations to the descendants of American slaves. When you combine these economic considerations with the horrors of the race riots, the hundreds of lynchings, the unjust court rulings, sharecropping, and Jim Crow laws, it is easy to understand why so many people are calling for reparations.

The real problem with reparations is not so much that they wouldn't help level the economic field of play, but rather that there is a big problem with their implementation. Why do people who were descendants of slave owners, but are perfectly decent people today, have to bear the economic responsibility for the sins of their fathers? In today's society there are no slaves and there are no slave owners, which makes it extremely difficult to determine who should pay and who should receive. Also, what percentage of Black blood would one have to have in order to make a claim? Would the remuneration be distributed based on percentage of Black blood, or just on the presence of Black bloodlines? What about the descendants of Blacks who were slave owners or were free? Should they be giving or receiving?

I don't think there is any reasonable person who would not acknowledge the fact that tremendous injustice was heaped upon Blacks in America historically. The question is, can that situation be rectified through some system that punishes the descendants of slave owners? It should be noted that the vast majority of whites in the South were not slave owners and would never have been able to afford slaves. Can you imagine how resentful the descendants of these individuals would be if their Black neighbors were receiving reparations and they were not, even though they were both at the same economic level? We are all very familiar with the phrase "Two wrongs don't make a right." In this case truer words were never spoken.

These kinds of stories certainly help us to understand why white guilt and Black victimhood have become so prevalent in our society and why it has become so easy for those with nefarious agendas to manipulate the various factions of our society into believing that they are enemies. You might say, what advantage is it to them to have Americans fighting each other and creating general chaos? Well, remember, if you want to fundamentally change a society, you must first want people who compose that society to desire change. They are not going to desire change if everything is rosy and peaceful. On the other hand, if everything seems to be deteriorating rather rapidly, a different system might potentially be better or at least might seem like a reasonable alternative.

When you combine white guilt and Black victimhood, you end up with proposals such as defunding the police, resegregating teaching facilities, unworkable reparations for slavery, and a host of things that sometimes even sound good on the surface but don't lead to unity and strength. Perhaps the most benign and potentially beneficial proposal emanating from guilt and victimhood was "affirmative action." This policy allowed government and nongovernmental entities to correct the underrepresentation in their organizations of certain groups based on race, sex, creed, national origin, and so on by enacting policies that provided preferential treatment in admissions and hiring procedures. At the time that affirmative action was first implemented, there were many whites who had not been around enough Blacks to realize that they are human beings like anyone else, who are just as capable as anyone else in any field of endeavor. Without affirmative action, that realization is not likely to have occurred; therefore, the outcome of that policy was positive on balance. The question is, how long should the preferential treatment go on?

Perhaps a better model would be something I call "compassionate action." We have always been a very compassionate nation, quite willing to lend a helping hand to those who are down on their luck. We want to give the underdog a fighting chance to achieve success. In a fair system, we should want to give every underdog a chance for success without respect to their race. Special consideration should be afforded based on a person's circumstances as opposed to their race. For example, as a neurosurgeon, I was extremely well compensated, and I also had other sources of revenue. My three sons all attended college and have done well in life. The question is, should they have been given preferential treatment during the college admissions process because they are Black? What about the white kid from West Virginia whose father was killed in a coal mine when he was eight years old and who has been working since he was twelve to help support his impoverished family? He reaches the 90th percentile on his SAT and has a 3.7 grade point average. This young man would clearly be much more disadvantaged than any of my sons even though he is white. In the compassionate action paradigm, he would be given extra consideration that might make the difference in terms of his admission and a potential scholarship. The beauty of this kind of system is that it caters to the most needy segment of the population. Currently, Blacks and Latinos would probably benefit most from the compassionate action plan, but twenty years from now it may be a different group. The bottom line is that extra consideration should be based on need and not skin color.

Previously a lot of the racial discrimination that took place in our country was based on ignorance rather than maliciousness. Once that ignorance was erased, the discriminatory behavior disappeared. When people behave unfairly out of ignorance, the faith-based principles of forgiveness should be on display. The guilty party is usually very appreciative of understanding and often will go out of their way to demonstrate that appreciation.

I vividly remember being an intern at Johns Hopkins starting in 1977. Black doctors in academic medical institutions were extremely rare at that time. When I appeared on some of the wards in scrubs, I was frequently mistaken for an orderly or occasionally a respiratory therapist. (Before I go on, I should state emphatically that there is nothing wrong with being an orderly or a respiratory therapist.) A nurse once said to me, "You are early. Mr. Johnson is not ready to be wheeled off to the operating room yet." I simply replied, "I'm sorry he's not ready, but I'm Dr. Carson and I'm here to see someone else." She turned eighteen shades of red with extreme embarrassment and I immediately knew that she felt horrible about her mistake. Rather than making her feel even worse, I told her not to feel bad and that I knew it was an innocent mistake and I was not offended in the least. I will tell you that that nurse became a friend for life. It is so much simpler to forgive and move on than it is to be easily offended and hold grudges. That does nothing good for either party.

Speaking of being offended, that is a big part of victimhood in modern society. When I gave the keynote speech at the National Prayer Breakfast in 2013, I stated that political correctness was very dangerous and could play a significant role in the destruction of our country if we allowed it to proliferate. I hate to say, "I told you so," but political correctness has assumed ridiculous importance in our communication mechanisms today. Because of this, people can lose their livelihood for simply using the wrong pronoun when innocently referring to another individual. We have not yet realized that political correctness can actually stifle free speech and the First Amendment. If people have to monitor every word they say for fear of consequences, then we certainly are not in a free-speech environment.

Some people say it's not really an infringement on the First Amendment because the government is not imposing speech restrictions or punishments for violation thereof. What those people do not realize is that if speech restrictions are imposed by big tech, the media, an educational institution, or an employer with the complicity of the federal government or local governments, the effect is the same as if the federal government imposed the speech restrictions. Our constitutional freedoms are essential to our identity as a free society. We must be on guard constantly for challenges to those essential freedoms.

One of the reasons that victimization is on the rise is that there are rewards for being a victim in today's society. I think we have all heard about the "safe spaces" on university campuses where students can hide without fear of someone saying something that will injure their delicate feelings. Some schools even have "trigger warnings" to alert students that there may be some material in the class that might prompt memories of some trauma they suffered in the past. Some schools will excuse students from those assignments or those classes. Is this wisdom, or insanity? The same students will have to go out into the real world and in many cases they may have to face competitors from other countries and other cultures who will eat them alive. We must absolutely cease attaching benefits to victimhood or it will inevitably continue to expand. I have no problem with appropriate trauma-informed care, but that care should seek to expose people to things that trouble them and teach them to cope with them rather than running away and hiding. It is always better to face challenges than to look for safe spaces unless one plans to be a hermit. Again, we should remember that it was the can-do attitude as opposed to the what-can-you-do-for-me attitude that made America great.

Perhaps one of the most pernicious and destructive policy ideas to come out of the guilt/victimhood ideological model is the concept of guaranteed basic income. In this model everyone gets a weekly, biweekly, or monthly check for hundreds or in some cases thousands of dollars in order to take care of all of their basic needs such as food and shelter. There is no requirement to obtain this funding other than being a living, breathing human being. This is the epitome of socialism and the antithesis of capitalism. Of course, if people are given everything they need to survive, many of them will be disinclined to seek employment.

It would be tantamount to extending CARES Act funding indefinitely. Because of such funding it has been extremely difficult for many small businesses to hire people who are willing to work as opposed to sitting at home collecting government checks that are funded by other hardworking Americans. There are few things that will destroy a well-functioning capitalistic society as quickly as widespread dependency on government aid. This kind of government support comes with a very high price tag and massively increases the national debt, which at some point will have to be dealt with rather than kicked down the road. Unfortunately for the next generations, it will become their problem, while the older people who are generating the problem will have died, completely oblivious or uncaring about the financial havoc their actions induced.

As we enact policies that create dependency on the government, we are also extinguishing the American dream. Because people will be compelled through taxation to combat the enormous national debt, there will be limited opportunities to accumulate the financial resources necessary to use the innovative entrepreneurial skills that have invigorated America in the past. It seems almost inconceivable that we have so rapidly reached the point where we are considering trading one of the highest standards of living in the world and almost unlimited opportunities for socialism cloaked as social justice.

If anyone doubts the results of trading a thriving capitalistic society for socialism, they need look no further than

Venezuela. I had an opportunity to visit Venezuela a number of times over the past couple of decades, and I must say that it was a pleasant place, with beautiful resorts, hotels, and shopping venues. The biggest issue the people argued about was whether or not they were the most beautiful people in the world. They had the best economy in South America and I was on the board of directors of an American company that had a thriving business there. There were many companies with thriving businesses that were providing great economic opportunities for the citizens of Venezuela. Now their socialistic government has created a nation from which the people are fleeing and that has one of the lowest standards of living in South America. That transition occurred within the space of a decade. There are definitely lessons to be learned by observant nations. Hopefully we will be one of them.

One minority group that we have not really discussed yet is Asians. Certainly, Asians have suffered significant discrimination in America historically. There were many unpleasant incidents involving Chinese railway workers during the construction of the transcontinental railroad, which was completed in 1869. During World War II, internment camps were demanded for Japanese Americans because people were distrustful of people of Japanese ancestry. They were shamefully treated for no other reason than the color of their skin. Now we have a problem with Asians being discriminated against at some of our high-powered, highly selective universities. Many such institutions are trying to limit the number of Asians because they do so well academically that using normal admissions criteria would yield classes that were very heavily populated with Asian students. Is it really fair to penalize people for doing too well? It certainly seems to go against the grain of "the American way." Rather than penalizing Asian students, wise educators would be studying them in order to raise the performance of non-Asian students. This is a no-brainer and is much more consistent with the American way. The sooner we realize that people are people and each one is entitled to being treated with respect, the sooner much friction will be dissipated among us.

After this lengthy discussion, it seems appropriate to ask whether there is a cure for white guilt or for minority victimhood in America. If there isn't, we are doomed. But we must remember that this is America, where the can-do spirit, although drenched, is still aflame. We remain one nation under God. We should seek wisdom from the source of wisdom not only in church or when we are in trouble, but constantly. In the Bible, Romans 8:1 tells us that there is no condemnation for those that are in Christ Jesus. That means that forgiveness is available for those who ask for it and are willing to strive to lead a good life. We do not have to let someone else decide whether we should feel guilt or shame for what was done by others at another time in history. The Bible also tells us that in order to be forgiven, we must be willing to forgive others.

A spirit of charity can bring a world of relief to a heart that has been embittered.

I believe the cure for victimhood is resiliency. We must be able to spring back when there has been a setback as opposed to giving up and accepting the role of victim. I told the story earlier of the time when some ruffians threatened to kill me if I continued to attend Wilson Junior High School, which was a white institution. I could easily have played the victim and heeded their warnings and transferred to another school. The alternative was to be resilient and determine that I would not allow them to control my future. I chose another route to school that was very public, which would likely preclude any blatant physical attacks. And even if it didn't, I was out to prove that I could outsmart my tormentors. Much of that resiliency was secondary to my faith, because I had prayed for protection, but I realized that I had to do my part by using my brain to avoid violence and mayhem.

Speaking of the brain, the way we think about those things in our environment has a great deal to do with whether we feel guilt or like victims. Case in point: We were taking a family vacation in Utah. My wife and I were commenting on the fact that after an entire day, we had not seen a single Black person other than ourselves. That wasn't a point of concern, but rather just an observation. That evening my three young sons and I visited a game arcade. I think the manager was so shocked to see Black people that he came over to us and gave us each a handful of game tokens, completely free of charge. He said, "You fellas have a good time on us." There are several ways that I could have interpreted his actions. I could have said, "What a nice man," and proceeded with the games. Or I could have been offended, concluding that he was an obvious racist who wanted us to have fun and then quickly vacate the premises. Or I could have thought that he was trying to keep us there so he could call his buddies to do us harm. Obviously, there are several other possibilities as well. The point here is that our realities are influenced by our perceptions. If we think someone is a racist, we interpret everything they say and do in light of our preconceived judgment. By the same token, if we think they are smart and fair, we might interpret the exact same actions in a very different way. As free moral agents, we each have the ability to influence our spheres of existence in a positive or a negative direction. We can be a victim or a victor. We can be guilt-ridden or happily guilt-free. We should never let others determine our state of being. By the way, my sons and I determined that the manager in the game arcade had nothing but the best of intentions and we made sure that he knew we really appreciated his gesture.

CHAPTER 5

Critical Race Theory and the 1619 Project

As previously mentioned, Vladimir Lenin, the Marxist revolutionary, once said, "Give me four years to teach the children and the seed I have sown will never be uprooted." He was not timid about revealing his plan to indoctrinate the next generations of his potential followers. Like many others, he understood how important it is to plant the seeds that help determine exactly who a person is while they are young and impressionable. Historical analysis demonstrates that one of the best ways to change society is to indoctrinate the population. We currently have a particularly dangerous situation in America because we have forces that want to fundamentally change our nation, coupled with powerful social media and power-hungry politicians. Some of our founders were not certain that we could maintain a free democratic republic over a long period of time. That is because there is a natural tendency for people to want to control their environment, including the thoughts and actions of everyone in that environment.

Our Constitution was specifically designed to thwart the attempts of government to take control of people's lives. It was also designed to leave most governmental policy issues in the hands of local officials who would owe their position to their voting constituents. This provides a much greater sense of checks and balances than does a system in which unelected Washington bureaucrats design policies that affect the entire population. It is of grave concern when those Washington bureaucrats and those they influence begin to push ideology that is contrary to the concept of God-given rights and liberty and justice for all. When the bureaucrats begin talking about righting past social injustices through government programs, alarm bells should go off. Not because we shouldn't be socially conscious, but rather because in a diverse society there is no uniform agreement on how to handle such issues. When those elected to powerful positions begin to use the tools available to them to impose their will on the populace by only exposing people to the things they want them to hear and shutting down opposing speech, we should be warned that suppression of freedom is imminent.

Critical race theory (CRT) is one of the ideological

pillars of the groups wanting to fundamentally change America. It is the child of critical legal studies, which tried to demonstrate that our legal system and laws were largely designed to protect the interest of rich and powerful white people at the expense of minorities and the economically less fortunate. Critical race theory advocates the same thing, but it also entails a belief that race is not a biologically natural entity but rather a social construct used to suppress people of color. CRT can be found advocating for the defunding of police and other socially destructive actions because its advocates think that legal institutions in the United States are all innately racist and are there to maintain a social order in which whites inhabit the superior positions. Since race is clearly genetically determined, it is difficult to understand their claim that it is only a social construct. There could be some nobility associated with their claim, since there is no real evidence of intellectual differences among different racial groups. Certainly, as a neurosurgeon, whenever I opened someone's skull and exposed their brain, their other physical characteristics no longer mattered. The brain, which is the same in all races, is really the thing that makes a person who they are, and all of our brains function in the same way and have the same neuroanatomical structure.

Critical race theory also claims that racism is normal in the United States of America. They say it is an integral part of all of our social infrastructure and that no minorities are exempt from its cruel consequences. As I have previously said, if you think a system is systemically racist, you will identify racism in every part of that society. There is a saying that "perception is reality," and that certainly is the case when one interprets everything based on their ideological belief system. Furthermore, the advocates of CRT believe that there are many intersections among the groups it advocates for. For instance, you could be a Black female homosexual. That intersectionality, in their opinion, should significantly increase your interest in their political viewpoints.

There are a host of other rabbit holes that we could explore given the voluminous accounts of what CRT is and isn't, but before moving on to talk about the 1619 Project, it should be mentioned that CRT believes that only people of color are its best and most legitimate spokespersons. I suspect that the advocates of CRT might find some real traction among the populace if, instead of trying to convince the impressionable children that they are either oppressors or oppressed, they focused on something that could be very beneficial to our society: closing the wealth gap. Currently the average white family in America has a net worth that is five to ten times greater than that of the average Black family. Some of that is because of historical conditions that did not allow for the accumulation of multigenerational wealth in Black families. Although the gap has shrunk in recent years, it still remains the source of much resentment and many grievances. Not having access to financial resources frequently negates the economic potential of the entrepreneurial spirit and innovative know-how. If some of the interest groups that are expending enormous energy trying to indoctrinate our children would devote a fraction of that time to finding ways to further close the economic gap, I suspect a much greater good for the society would be realized.

Perhaps even more good could be done if the energies of the groups seeking fundamental change in America were focused on inner cities like Chicago, where an inordinate number of people are shot and killed every weekend. It's worse than the Wild West, where at least the sheriff had the support of local officials in fighting violent crime. It is appalling that groups like Black Lives Matter are virtually silent when it comes to innocent Black lives in these large cities. If we want to talk about racism, let's talk about the fact that if dozens of lives were being taken in certain well-heeled communities in our nation, there would be a tremendous outcry. But since it's Black people killing other Black people in some of these progressive cities, the same people who were crying "racism" about virtually everything occurring in our society remain curiously silent. What about all the cries for equity of outcome for everyone? Where is the equity of outcome for all those young people in Chicago who are being slaughtered, and why does no one care?

The 1619 Project tries to rewrite American history

with the consequences of slavery and the contributions of African Americans at the center. This was a project initiated by the *New York Times*, whose goal was to advocate that the introduction of African slaves to America was the nation's true origin, as opposed to our Declaration of Independence from Britain. The project also wanted to establish slavery and its resulting consequences as foundational pillars of American society. It claims that the year 1619, which denotes the first arrival of Africans as slaves to America, should be seen as the beginning of the history of this country rather than 1776, when we declared our independence from Great Britain and started forming autonomous policies. As was seen in chapter 3, the first slaves probably actually arrived in the 1500s. Slavery was horrendous and cannot be excused in any way, but proponents of the 1619 Project seem to portray America as somehow more evil than all the other civilizations where slavery existed.

There has been evidence of slavery since the beginning of recorded history, and again, it was horrible, but America is not unique in having utilized the labor of others for its own economic advantage. America was unique, however, in that it had so many people who were morally outraged that an institution like slavery could exist in our country, with its Judeo-Christian foundation, that they were willing to go to war and sacrifice a substantial portion of the population to end the practice. Some will say the war was not about ending slavery, but rather preserving the Union.

A more in-depth analysis would quickly reveal that the reason for the secession of the South was so that it could maintain slavery. This is "elementary, my dear Watson."

There were plenty of culprits responsible for the slave trade in the Americas, and not all of them were of European ancestry. In Africa, like everywhere else, there were wars and conquests. It was not unusual for the defeated tribes to be taken as slaves if they were not executed. When the opportunity presented itself to sell such individuals for a handsome profit, there was no hesitation, and voilà, the transatlantic slave trade materialized. It is important for people to realize that Africans sold other Africans into slavery. And the Europeans would have had little success capturing Africans on their home turf without substantial assistance from other Africans.

Speaking of others who were involved in the evil institution of slavery, many people do not know that in America there were Black slave owners, many of whom owned white slaves. This is documented in many places, including an excellent essay by the former chairman of the department of African American studies at Harvard, Dr. Henry Louis Gates.[1] In 1670 the Virginia House of Burgesses forbade Blacks and Indians from purchasing "Christian" slaves. This prohibition was enshrined as law thirty-five years later. As I previously mentioned, "Christians" was a euphemism for white. Many people also do not realize that there were free Blacks in the South just as there were in the North and that many of them were extremely prosperous.

It was the sense of entitlement on behalf of many whites that created problems for such Blacks because many whites did not feel that Blacks should be able to obtain wealth in a "white nation."

I bring all this up to emphasize the point that people are people. Their race doesn't matter if they are able to obtain an advantage over others, and many of them are driven by avarice and other nefarious motives. This is why it is so important to evaluate people based on their character and what they do, rather than on their physical characteristics, over which they have no control. That feeling of white entitlement that occurred so long ago in our nation is one of the root causes of so-called white privilege today. However, today, just like in those days, there are many whites who don't feel entitled to what someone else has worked for, and therefore it is undeniably unfair to group all whites into the category of oppressors, as critical race theory and the 1619 Project try to do.

One of our biggest problems in America right now is the tendency to allow social media to dictate the terms of our morality. They, along with extreme left-leaning segments of our society, feel that they can dictate all definitions and meanings, including who is a racist. If they were honest, I think their analysis would lead them right to the mirror. What could be more racist than trying to ascribe to individuals certain ideological beliefs just because of the color of their skin? If people don't adhere to your definition of what they should believe, then they are abused with all types of slurs on their character. Fair-minded people obviously do not engage in castigating other people for their beliefs, but far too many of those people just stand in the corner with their heads down saying nothing in the hope that no one will call them a nasty name. This is not the kind of courage that leads to the persistence of "the land of the free."

In light of the 1619 Project discussion, it cannot be overemphasized that slavery has been a part of human civilization since time immemorial. If America is to be demonized for the practice of slavery, so should every other society where it has been practiced. This is barely mentioned by the progressives who want to fundamentally change our society because it doesn't fit the narrative of America having a systemically racist infrastructure. If in fact we have that, then all the other societies that have engaged in slavery would seem to have it also.

It is hard to imagine the cognitive dissonance that must have existed among the slave owners who also proclaimed themselves God-fearing Christians. One would have to have a very strong sense of rationalization to justify holding another human being against their will and subjecting them to harsh treatment and often subhuman living conditions. This would have become particularly difficult after the time when slaves developed facility with the English language and could express themselves. Many slave owners benefited by owning slaves who were innovative and skillful, with many displaying expert craftsmanship. Many of the slaves were far more talented than their masters, and yet they had to be subject to the will of many unkind individuals who in most cases saw no reason to share the profits with those responsible for them. This is not to say that there were not some kind slave owners, but in a way that is an oxymoron, because if they were truly kind, they would have freed the slaves and given them some money or property to support themselves until they became self-sufficient. A sense of right and wrong that leads one to do what is right would have made it very difficult to be a slave owner. Many tried to assuage that guilt by telling themselves that the slaves were better off on a plantation in America than they would have been trying to escape hungry lions in the jungles of Africa.

It is extremely politically incorrect for a Black person to say that they are better off in America than they would have been in Africa. Although I am not politically correct, I do try to avoid being extremely so when possible. I will simply say that I praise God all the time for allowing me to be born an American with tremendous opportunities and a great deal of freedom. I have had the pleasure of visiting sixty-eight countries and living overseas, and I can honestly say, "There is no place like home." We have a long-standing Constitution that is designed to protect and preserve our liberties and ensure just treatment for everyone. Does it do those things perfectly in every case? Of course not, because it was written by imperfect people and has to be enforced by imperfect people. I would, however, challenge anyone to show me a nation that provides better opportunities for its people and displays a greater sense of morality.

People came to our shores from every part of the world and from every nationality seeking the promise of self-determination and freedom. Regardless of their nation of origin, they became Americans. Whether they came of their free will or involuntarily, they became Americans. Through the united strength of all those people, this nation became the predominant power of the entire world. It is because of the common interest and destiny of all these people that we have garnered enormous strength and influence and have been able to provide a better existence for people in many other nations. Before America became the greatest power in the world, despotic leaders commonly crushed and looted other weaker nations. Because of America's example and power, other nations tend to behave themselves to a much greater degree than previously. If the United States of America relinquishes that influence through ineptitude by its political leaders, all of humanity will suffer the consequences.

I just gave one example of the tremendous good seen throughout the world due to the existence of the United States of America. It would be just as easy to give an example of something untoward caused by our country. When it comes to teaching our children about our history, we can, as some have already demonstrated, choose to emphasize only the negative aspects and minimize the positive and inspiring portions, or we can choose to give a balanced and objective comprehensive view that will show a very impressive historical picture. Clearly the proponents of CRT and the 1619 Project have chosen to emphasize the negative in order to enhance their ideological views. They have every right to espouse this negativity, but it is very important that their philosophical views be kept in perspective and not be presented as the only choice without alternative views in our nation's classrooms. In no way am I advocating that we gloss over the issue of slavery in our educational institutions. It is a very important part of our history and its consequences are still being felt today. Wise people learn from their history, even the negative aspects thereof, but foolish people try to bury or rewrite their history to suit their ideological and philosophical comfort zones.

It breaks my heart to think about the slave families that were torn apart when children were taken away from their parents and sold, frequently to masters who lived far away or in other states, precluding the possibility of visitation or even ever seeing their beloved family members again. Perhaps even more difficult for slave families was to be subjected to watching people for whom they cared deeply being beaten, raped, and in some cases even murdered with little or no recourse.

Clearly many of the slave masters were concerned about the possibility of a slave revolt. This was particularly the case in states like Mississippi and Alabama where in some areas slaves significantly outnumbered their oppressors.

The owners cleverly devised schemes to limit communication between some of the slaves, and they planted seeds of discord by telling the house slaves that they were better than the yard slaves and the yard slaves that they were better than the field slaves. Unfortunately, those seeds of discord continued to germinate even after slavery ended, because it was still necessary to keep the Black population divided in order for whites to maintain their power and their societal control. One of the mechanisms they used was to convince light-skinned Blacks that they were better than those of medium complexion and to convince the ones of medium complexion that they were better than those of dark complexion.

Amazingly, the sequelae of those falsehoods still linger today among some groups of Blacks. One might be tempted to say the attempts to keep the Black community divided are relics of our dark past and fortunately have disappeared from our view. It would be wonderful if that were true, but it is not. Even today there are entities in our society that are sowing seeds of discord in the Black community to prevent a united front from discovering how much power it could have. They do this by attempting to convince the majority of Blacks that anyone who does not adhere to certain progressive agendas is a race traitor or an Uncle Tom. This keeps a large number of Black Americans from even considering alternative viewpoints of what they should think and how they should conduct themselves. They are told who they should admire and who they should abhor and certainly who they should vote for. Even though the peer pressure is enormous, increasing numbers of Black Americans are thinking for themselves and analyzing the data, which allows them to make decisions based on actual evidence and not just what someone has told them.

When it comes to an issue like poverty, the progressive view is that there is a disproportionate prevalence of it in the Black community primarily because racist white people have enacted policies to suppress Black advancement and guarantee continued oppression by whites. Interestingly enough, an in-depth study of poverty by the Brookings Institution,[2] which, by the way, is hardly conservative, demonstrated that the incidence of poverty in one's life could be reduced to the 3 percent range if one did the following:

- Finish high school
- Get married
- Wait until one is married before having children
- Get a job

It didn't matter what the racial background of the person was as long as they followed these guidelines, which once were commonly known in America. What is really being said by these guidelines? "Finish high school" is emphasizing the incredible importance of having a solid educational foundation in order to take advantage of the abundant opportunities that surround every person in an environment such as we have in America. Anyone from any background can virtually write their own ticket if they have a solid educational foundation. They tend to express themselves in a way that commands attention, and their expressed knowledge base demands attention to their words.

"Get married" draws attention to the importance of developing strong familial bonds. When navigating the many obstacles encountered while living in a complex society, there are few things more valuable than dependable individuals who will support you unconditionally in all your endeavors. During my career as a neurosurgeon, I can remember coming home on many occasions and feeling extremely exhausted and/or discouraged. Sometimes I wonder what I would have done without a tender, loving wife who would comfort me during those times. Having people who are in your corner regardless of what is going on cannot be overvalued.

"Wait until one is married before having children" emphasizes the importance of planning ahead rather than just acting and reacting. Also, that kind of planning will likely result in a more stable financial situation in which to raise a child. Carelessly having children without the time and resources to care for them is extremely unfair to the child as well as to the society as a whole. Similarly, just cruising through life without a care and just reacting to things as they happen is a terrible waste of a sophisticated brain that was designed for complex long-range strategy execution.

"Get a job" is simply saying that work bestows upon the worker skills that are quite marketable and ultimately provide much more independence. Sitting at home and collecting government checks may seem to some like a way of gaming the system, but ultimately it is just gaming oneself because that individual is losing out on so many opportunities that only come with working. Also, the sense of self-worth is greatly magnified when one is self-supporting.

Many people think that the United States of America is impregnable with respect to the overthrow of its capitalistic society and the imposition of socialism or communism. There have been many others who also thought that their system of governance was fortified against Marxist domination. People would do well to remember how quickly the Soviet Union dissolved and how quickly Venezuela went from the most prosperous to the poorest nation in South America in a very short period of time. Once the erosion of freedom begins, its progression is frequently like a blitzkrieg. People are left wondering what happened. Before we suffer the loss of the precious freedoms that we currently enjoy, we must awaken to the slippery slopes of Marxist tendencies that are cropping up everywhere.

Very notably, we have attempts by many government officials to impose mandates for mask wearing and for getting vaccinated against COVID-19 and its variants. I am not opposed to vaccines, and I obviously wore masks every day during my surgical career, but I believe the American people are smart enough to do the right thing if they are given appropriate information in an honest way. They become suspicious when the government pushes nonscientific mandates on them. For instance, a Cleveland Clinic study and an Israeli study have clearly demonstrated that the natural immunity achieved after having contracted the COVID-19 virus is at least as good as and probably is much better than the immunity achieved after vaccination. Not only are the CDC and federal government officials failing to recognize this, but they are actively pushing people who already have achieved natural immunity to get vaccinated without providing an adequate explanation for such a recommendation. If we don't know the long-term risks of the vaccine and at the same time we know that people who have already had the virus are covered, why would you subject them to possible future problems when they are already protected? Could it be that there is a desire on behalf of many in the government to see just how far they can control the behavior of the populace just by putting forth mandates with no scientific backup? (Of course, everyone's medical situation is different and you should consult with your own medical doctor about the vaccines.)

We must remember that the government is not necessarily evil because it is trying to extend its power. That's what governing bodies do historically, and that is the reason why our founders were so meticulous about the way they wrote our Constitution. They wanted to prevent the gradual encroachment on our rights by a well-meaning but misguided government that only wanted power and forgot that the original intent was to let the country be of, by, and for the people.

The introduction of CRT into the classrooms of America has so far done little more than cause friction. It is antithetical to the dream of Dr. King, which was to reach a point in our nation where people were judged not on the color of their skin but on the content of their character. CRT would have our young people believe that their skin color is the principal determinant of their future. Can you imagine what life must be like for little children going to school where they and everyone else have to wear a mask? They fail to learn to correlate facial expressions with verbal communication. This is a substantial disadvantage when engaging in social interactions with other individuals. On top of that, they are told that they may be harboring a horrible disease and that even though they don't feel bad, they might transmit that disease to their elderly grandmother and kill her. When the grandmother dies of whatever cause, that young person is now feeling guilty. On top of that, if you are white, you are an oppressor, as are your relatives and ancestors, and you are responsible for the difficulties often encountered in our society by minorities. If you are Black, you are told that you are a victim of a society that is designed to maintain white power and white privilege. Furthermore, you are told that you will always be at a disadvantage because the system you live in is systemically racist. All of this is happening while our young people are trying to develop their self-image. If all of that confusion is not enough, they are then told that they may not actually be a girl or a boy. How can we possibly expect our young people to develop normally under these circumstances? To me, it seems like child abuse.

Childhood is supposed to be a happy time when young people begin to realize the tremendous potential that lies within them. It's a time when the imagination blossoms and gives birth to inspiring dreams that provide the drive and impetus to make those dreams come true. There is no better place than America to make that happen. Just because a child is born as a member of a racial minority and without a great deal of financial resources doesn't mean that they can't dream and achieve like anyone else. That is, unless they have been convinced that the color of their skin will preclude their ultimate success. That is why what some are doing to our children by robbing them of their dreams and their drive is akin to child abuse.

Many progressives cling to the narrative that America is a systemically racist country, claiming that there has not been great socioeconomic progress made by Black Americans in recent decades. It's not clear to me where these people have been hiding their heads, because one would not have to be very observant to realize that, just in my lifetime, the achievements of Blacks have been phenomenal. We now have Black generals and admirals as well as CEOs of Fortune 500 companies and presidents of prestigious universities, including Ivy League universities. We have had a Black president elected twice and have elected a Black vice president. I think it is fair to say that a Black child can now aspire to virtually any position in our society. This is not to say that we have solved all of our racial issues, but it is okay to acknowledge the fact that we have made enormous progress. There is still more work to be done, and it will be accomplished with much more facility if we focus on our successes and try to enhance those rather than just focusing on negativity, which is very divisive.

Can you imagine how boring the world would be if we all looked alike, with no variation? How many people would like to go and visit the zoo if all the animals there were Thomson's gazelles? Who would want to go to the aquarium if every fish were a goldfish? Who would want a bouquet of flowers if every one of them were identical? And who would want to get up in the morning if everybody looked exactly like you? Variety is a blessing from God. Leave it to evil forces to take that blessing and try to make it into a curse. We do not have to succumb to the forces of evil that try to divide us at every level. They try to create tension based on race, religion, age, income, political affiliation, sex, and any demographic they can think of. We have all heard the phrase "divide and conquer." Our nation is much too strong to be brought down by Russia or China or North Korea or Iran, or any other nation, for that matter. But we most certainly can be destroyed from within. As Jesus said, "A house divided against itself cannot stand."

Speaking of standing, I am delighted to see that there are parent groups all over the country standing up to the school boards that are pushing critical race theory and other divisive ideas on our children. It is these kinds of brave individuals, who are willing to suffer the slings and arrows of outrageous media and political forces, who will lead the charge in determining if life, liberty, and the pursuit of happiness continue to thrive in America.

CHAPTER 6

The George Floyd Turning Point

On May 25, 2020, a tragic incident occurred that sent shock waves across the globe. The police were called about a forty-six-year-old Black man by the name of George Floyd who was suspected of passing counterfeit money. Four police officers arrived and restrained Mr. Floyd and placed him in handcuffs. While he was cuffed, for reasons that are not clear, he was pulled from the police vehicle and placed on the ground, where Officer Derek Chauvin pressed his knee against Mr. Floyd's neck, pinning him to the ground and obstructing his airways. After more than nine minutes in this position, the prisoner expired. The incident was caught on a cell phone camera by a bystander and made available to the media, where it immediately went viral across the globe. Just prior to his death the prisoner uttered the words "I can't breathe." Those words became a signature chant around the world as protests in many cases morphed into violent and destructive riots. Dozens of people were killed and billions of dollars of damage was sustained.

One of the most shocking aspects of the incident was the totally emotionless face of that officer, who had the steely, cold eyes of a shark. That image made him appear to be callous and uncaring about the man he was in the process of killing before the world. Prior to that incident, many progressives had been proclaiming the presence of systemic racism against Blacks throughout the law enforcement community. They claimed that Black people were frequently mistreated by the police and were not only brutalized but were frequently killed without cause. Those, of course, are very serious charges and they require evidence before they are endowed with the gravitas necessary for in-depth investigations and action. Now, finally, progressives had very emotional video evidence to back up their claims. The video was shown incessantly and accompanied by commentary suggesting that this kind of brutality on behalf of the police was commonplace and required immediate intervention of local authorities to limit the power and scope of the police. Calls for defunding the police, which had previously been muffled, were now shouted from the mountaintops.

The claims of systemic racism in law enforcement were further enhanced when the background investigation of Derek Chauvin revealed a pattern of abusive behavior that could have been justification for discipline or dismissal even before this case occurred. Many on the left claimed that this officer was not an anomaly, but in fact represented typical police behavior. In this case, they argued, we were just fortunate to have captured the incident on video. The feeding frenzy among left-leaning news organizations was unprecedented in its magnitude. It was the subject of commentary on outlets such as CNN morning, noon, and night. The coverage was in no way objective and largely demonized law enforcement to the extent that there were massive protests in Europe as well as other countries throughout the world.

I was as disturbed as anyone looking at those video images of a fellow human being having his life slowly extinguished by another human being who appeared to have no compassion. The other officers on the scene appeared to be complicit, and the bystanders could do nothing but implore the police to cease this abusive behavior before the tragedy occurred. Even though I was disturbed, I have had many encounters with police and have never in all those episodes seen anything that even approached this level of inhumanity. We all know that there are rotten cops just as there are rotten doctors, rotten teachers, rotten journalists, and rotten individuals of virtually every occupation. The officer who committed this crime was beyond rotten. He was way off on the distal end of the bell curve in terms of behavior. There was virtually no one trying to justify his actions that day. Therefore, the attempts by the media to portray his actions as typical, although successful, were blatantly dishonest. They could not, however, have been more perfect as a mechanism to bolster the arguments for systemic racism in law enforcement.

As I previously mentioned, growing up in Detroit and Boston, I had numerous interactions with police officers. Like many people in disadvantaged neighborhoods, I found the police to be a source of comfort, because there were violent people around who would be even more violent and out of control without a police presence. This fact creates cognitive dissonance for many in minority communities who need the police but are constantly fed propaganda about how evil and racist they are. This is not to say that there are not some police officers who are racists, just as there are some teachers, nurses, electricians, and others who are racists, but for some strange reason we have more of a tendency to generalize about police than we do about other occupations. I believe that if we stop generalizing about police and see them as individuals, a lot of animosity could be avoided.

I was engaged in a conversation with a senior police officer in Baltimore not long ago, and he said he walks the same beat every day and knows everyone in the neighborhood and everyone knows him. He says he never has to buy lunch, because everyone is always inviting him in for lunch or snacks. Because he knows the neighborhood so well, he knows when something is not right, and people feel comfortable informing him about such things. He plays ball with the kids and is on a first-name basis with most of the adults. This is the kind of community policing that is effective and should be replicated throughout our nation.

During my senior year at Yale, I had a job as a student aide for the Yale police. It was fun working with the fully trained police staff, who became good friends and colleagues. They were like anyone else and took their jobs very seriously. It was fun riding along with them to see how cases were investigated and how they interacted with witnesses and suspects. They were always courteous and kind but also knew when toughness was required. The same was true of the Secret Service and the Federal Protective Service staff who safeguarded me during my run for president and as secretary of HUD. The latter were like members of the family and we would gladly do anything for any of them. The point is, the police are like anyone else, with the same joys and sorrows, and they too have feelings. We must resist those who attempt to demonize all of them and dehumanize them in order to make their mistreatment more acceptable.

If we are to achieve peace between police and minority communities, it will be necessary to actually look at the facts and remove emotion from the conversation. Anytime an unarmed member of the community is killed by police, it is a highly emotionally charged situation. It is easy to fan the flames of that emotion and create dangerous tensions that can result in property damage, looting, riots, and violence, including death. The victims, who are sometimes innocent and sometimes not, are virtually always lionized, while the police are most often demonized. Because of the breathless, almost incessant coverage of such incidents, most people believe that the killing of unarmed Black men by police is a common occurrence. Of course, the death of anyone is a tragedy, and regardless of what that individual was doing, they are still the son of some heartbroken mother, the father of some heartbroken child, or the sibling or friend of other heartbroken individuals in the community. That said, many public surveys have shown that most people, when asked how many unarmed Black men are killed by police annually, vastly overestimate the numbers, believing that the answer is in the hundreds or even a thousand or more. In 2019, various law enforcement databases indicated that the number is probably less than two dozen, while the number of police encounters annually is in the millions. In fact, in the year 2018 there were 61.5 million civilian contacts with police. Two dozen is still too many (the *Washington Post* database puts the number at less than a dozen), but it is not suggestive of widespread systemic racism. Significantly more police officers were killed during that same period, but with relatively little attention by the media.

We have to be realistic enough to recognize that if people engage in certain types of dangerous activities, such as armed robbery, gang violence, selling narcotics, human trafficking, and so on, they are much more likely to be involved in fatal officer-involved incidents. Depending on which data one analyzes and whether they do multivariant analyses or only look at one factor, you can prove almost any point, and therefore we should also integrate common sense into the analysis. For instance, if you asked the question "How many people who are being arrested for a crime are killed by police?" you would get a very different answer if you separated into two different categories those who resisted arrest and those who did not. Some would say that question introduces the negative aspect of blaming the victim. Could it be that in some cases the victims should be blamed? There would not be many cases where someone who was completely cooperative would be brutalized or killed by police.

Having said that, it is also important to recognize that many of the people who get into trouble that requires police intervention are inebriated or on drugs, which impairs their cognitive abilities and inhibitions, making them far more dangerous and more likely to elicit forceful countermeasures by law enforcement authorities. Some of these individuals are perfectly reasonable, law-abiding citizens when they are not under the influence of mind-altering substances. Even though they may be obnoxious, police are trained to be patient with them and to exercise restraint. With millions of police/citizen interactions annually and only a dozen or two fatalities caused by police, that training is obviously quite effective.

The issue of police accountability is a very sticky one, with multiple opinions coming from lots of different directions. In many states, for medical issues there exist physician review boards consisting of fellow physicians, legal experts, and ordinary citizens. They frequently work in conjunction with licensing boards, and this level of oversight largely eliminates quacks who practice a very dangerous brand of medicine. I believe something of that nature would provide the public with an oversight mechanism that would alleviate a lot of anxiety about rogue cops who repeatedly exhibit abusive behavior. Again, rogue cops may not be a common problem, but the havoc they create cannot be overestimated and therefore the goal should be to eliminate such behavior.

In a perfect world where the intentions of people are clearly understood, it is likely that incidents involving resisting the police and subsequent claims of brutality would be significantly dissipated. When people enter a situation with a certain mindset, they are likely to interpret what is happening or what is said in a way consistent with their preconceived notions. For instance, if you saw a young Black man walking on your property and holding a gun, what would be your reaction?

Twenty years ago, we purchased a farm in Upperco, Maryland, which is a very rural area outside of Baltimore.

Ben, the shortest one, with his brother, Curtis, and cousins, circa 1956.

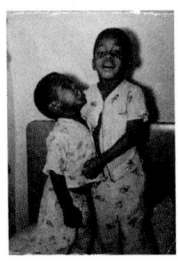

Ben with his brother, Curtis, circa 1954.

Ben as a high schooler in 1969.

Ben (wearing glasses in middle) as an officer in high school ROTC in 1969.

Ben's graduation from the University of Michigan Medical School in 1977.

Ben with his mother, Sonya, in 1985.

Ben as a young doctor at Johns Hopkins in 1985.

Ben's mom, Sonya, with her grandsons in 1987.

Ben and Candy's three sons in 2003.

Ben and Candy honoring General Colin Powell at a Carson Scholars Fund awards ceremony in 2009.

Candy's grandmother's graduation picture from nursing school at Meharry in 1924. She is fourth from the left.

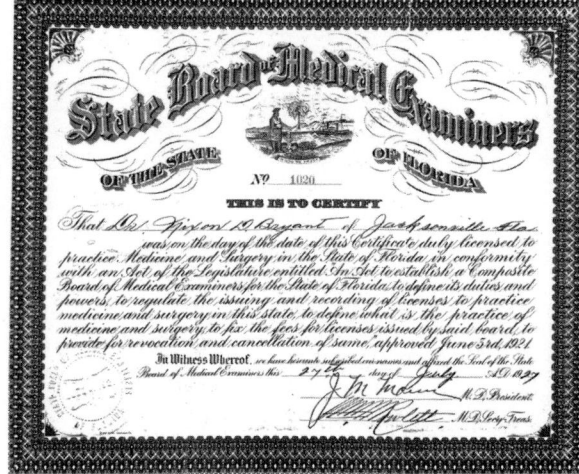

Candy's grandad Dr. Nixon D. Bryant's medical license, issued by the Florida State Board of Medical Examiners in July of 1927.

Ben having fun with his cutout during the 2016 presidential campaign.

The Carson family at the White House in 2017.

Ben in his Washington, DC, office at the Department of Housing and Urban Development, circa 2019.

Ben with Andrew Hughes, his chief of staff at HUD, circa 2020.

Ben and Candy ringing the closing bell at the New York Stock Exchange in 2018.

In 2019 on the way to a conference where both were speaking, Vice President Mike Pence and Ben surprised Candy with cupcakes on Air Force Two, since it was her birthday.

Ben with Dr. Carla Hayden, also of Baltimore, the first female and Black American to serve as librarian of Congress, in 2019.

Ben, with Candy, speaking at the opening of a new HUD EnVision Center, circa 2019.

Ben speaking about the new think tank/do tank American Cornerstone Institute in 2021.

Ben III is held by his dad, Ben Jr., and joined by both grandfathers in 2020.

Carson family photo in 2017.

Ben and Candy in 2020.

Rhoeyce, our youngest son, was fourteen years old and went exploring while carrying his pellet gun, which looked like an ordinary rifle. We never raised him to be fearful or paranoid about the potential actions of others based on his race. We were quite stunned when a pickup truck pulled up in front of our house carrying Rhoeyce. It was a neighbor who lived over a mile away on another farm, who informed us that she had seen Rhoeyce walking in a field with a rifle and recognized that he was in grave danger. We thanked her for her kindness and immediately had a talk with our son about rural etiquette. We wanted to be sure that he understood that it would be very unusual in that neck of the woods to see a young Black man walking around with a rifle on private property. There are some people who would simply ignore him, there are others who would inform him that he was on private property, and there might even be a few who would react violently and out of fear.

Maybe my son should have felt free in a free country to walk around with a rifle and not fear repercussions, but the wisdom that frequently accompanies aging would dictate that that is not a good idea. If, God forbid, he had been shot or injured by a fearful resident, I suspect that there would have been many cries of rural racism, or perhaps not since he was the son of a conservative Black person. Many progressives are not particularly concerned about the rights of conservative Blacks or conservative women, and you rarely hear a peep from them when the rights of such individuals are compromised. Let's hope and pray that one day their hearts will be touched by a desire to be fair to everyone.

This story about my youngest son may seem frightening to some, but it also contains some encouraging elements about our society. The fact that a neighbor whom we had never met cared deeply about the welfare of a young man of a race different from hers indicates that our stereotypes of racist rural residents may not be justified. In fact, we have met some of the nicest people we have ever known in Upperco. Once, after a massive snowfall that left forty inches of snow on the ground and drifts that were much higher, a neighbor who owned a heavy equipment business cleared our drive from the main road, which was more than three-quarters of a mile away, without charge. In another instance, we were having some pallets of marble delivered from Canada in a big eighteen-wheeler. Unfortunately, they had forgotten to load a forklift, without which it was impossible to unload the truck. A neighbor with a forklift came to our aid, again without charge. These are just a couple of the multitudinous kind deeds and kind people that we encountered in rural Maryland. Are there some people who are not kind and considerate of others in the area? The answer to that is, of course there are. This is why it is so important to recognize that people are people and we should evaluate them not on the color of their skin but rather on who they are as a person. That is the reason that God endowed us with significant intellectual capacity. If we only had to evaluate and react to external physical characteristics, we would need a brain no more sophisticated than that of most animals.

Even though police are trained to quickly evaluate potentially dangerous situations and act appropriately, they are human beings and also are subject to preconceived notions that can impact their actions. I say this not to excuse mistakes that they sometimes make, but rather to emphasize the importance of recognizing them as fellow human beings and perhaps teaching our young people that the police are deserving of their respect and cooperation. When they are treated with respect and cooperation, the likelihood of a violent encounter dramatically decreases.

Interestingly, in 2016 there was another case that bore many similarities to the George Floyd case. It was the case of Tony Timpa. He suffered from schizophrenia and had called the police himself because he was concerned about his behavior, having missed taking his medications. He ended up being restrained by three police officers, including a knee to the back of his neck pinning him to the ground. This went on for fourteen minutes before he expired. Before his death he was heard pleading, "You're gonna kill me." The case got very little attention compared to the Floyd case, perhaps because Mr. Timpa was white and his situation did not promote the narrative of systemic racism. The case does clearly indicate a need for police accountability since none of the officers involved were charged or dismissed. A judge ruled that they were protected by "qualified immunity." This is the reason why so many have been calling for the elimination of qualified immunity. It was perhaps a misinterpretation of how qualified immunity should be used. Obviously, police need some protection from frivolous lawsuits every time they carry out their duties. This is an issue that needs serious in-depth study and a real legal solution instead of cursory conversation periodically when cases like this emerge. Again, the behavior of the police in this case was not typical, and we must be careful not to make inappropriate judgments about whole classes of people based on aberrant behavior by a small segment.

There always seems to be a rush to judgment in these high-profile cases in which there appears to be inappropriate police behavior. This is not surprising since the irresponsible news media not only incessantly report the case without having all the facts, but also provide very judgmental commentary. They are frequently the agents that spread falsehoods that are very difficult to subsequently eradicate. For instance, in the case of Breonna Taylor, it was widely rumored that the police were at the wrong house and used a "no-knock warrant."[1] Neither of those things were true. It was further rumored that the police started the firefight, which also was not true (Taylor's boyfriend admitted that).

One of the biggest lies was that she was lying in her bed when she was shot. The investigation found that was completely untrue. These kinds of falsehoods can be quickly spread but are very difficult to take back. Many who have a specific agenda that includes dividing people take advantage of that fact.

In dealing with police, I have noticed that they have a special bond between them, perhaps because they are putting their lives on the line every day and putting their families through incredible stress every time that phone rings. They also see each other being demonized not only by the press but often by the mayor and city council and city prosecutors. Just like soldiers fighting together in a foxhole, they make it a point of having each other's back. This is the reason for the difficulty in getting police officers to testify against one of their own even when they know a wrong has been committed. When a police officer is aware of inappropriate activity committed by another officer, they must listen to their higher angels and report the wrongdoing. I realize that this is much easier said than done, but it is a matter of integrity and honor. In the beginning, the peer pressure to keep silent will be enormous. If a consistent pattern of integrity is demonstrated, the covert incidents of unrighteous behavior will gradually disappear, as will some of the animosity between law enforcement agents and the community. The bad apples can only operate when they are being shielded by their colleagues. If good cops stop protecting bad cops, the bad cops will either change their ways or move on.

As one can see from this discussion, all of the bad behavior is not on one side or the other. There's plenty of blame to go around. When one of these highly publicized but rare incidents occurs where a police officer shoots and kills an unarmed Black man, there is highly predictable rage leading to violence and mayhem and sometimes even death. Why is the anger so vehement? Perhaps the answer is found in cases like that of Rayshard Brooks, a twenty-seven-year-old Black man who fell asleep in his car at a Wendy's drive-through in Atlanta. The police were summoned and attempted to arrest Brooks after he failed a sobriety test. Brooks was able to seize the Taser from one of the officers and fled with one officer in hot pursuit. That officer subsequently shot him several times in the back, resulting in his demise. The officer was subsequently fired and has been charged with second-degree murder.

A lot of the anger in this case stems from the fact that Brooks was running away from the officers and not posing a threat to them. They had his car and his identification information and could easily have subsequently arrested him at his home or elsewhere. The question being asked by so many is, why did they have to kill a young man for resisting arrest and running away, knowing who he was and how to find him later? There are those who would say his life was not valuable enough to the police officer who shot him. On the other side there are many who have said that Brooks would be alive today if he had not resisted arrest and fled. Still others would say that if Brooks had been white, this would not have happened. I'm not sure that is true since, in doing some research for this book, I found several cases in which white men were killed by the police for questionable infractions. But these cases got little or no attention because they didn't fit the narrative of systemic racism.

The Brooks case clearly should not have ended with the death of a young man with bad judgment. At the same time, police cannot be expected to turn a blind eye to individuals who are breaking the law. It seems that there is room for discussion of nonlethal restraint methods rather than the traditional teaching that when police use a gun, they shoot to kill. Necessity is the mother of invention, and we are a very creative nation. Therefore, with the appropriate emphasis, I suspect we could arm our police officers with some nonlethal alternatives fairly quickly. There are already some police departments around the country that are experimenting with restraint systems like BolaWrap. This is a gun-like apparatus that fires a projectile with Kevlar-based string that instantly wraps the target securely without causing pain. It can be deployed from a distance of more than twenty feet, reducing the likelihood of a scuffle that could produce injuries. More important, looking for these alternative restraint measures sends the message that we value the lives of all our citizens and will go to great lengths to avoid unnecessary loss of life. It is not reasonable, however, to expect police to put their own lives at risk during an arrest attempt in which the suspect has the ability to quickly deploy lethal force. Progressive forces must come to understand that when they give unconditional support to violent criminals, they are actually hurting that person's chances of long-term survival. Because criminal behavior that is not punished severely will only continue to grow and eventually cost the life of its perpetrator.

Before demonizing the police, it might be instructive to imagine what our society would be like without them. This is an intellectual exercise that those who advocate the defunding of police have obviously not engaged in. Everyone would have to be armed and ready to defend their families and their property and we would once again replicate the Wild West. Someone could walk into your house and say, "I like that television. I think I will take it. Better still, I like this house, so you get out and I will live here." In other words, civil society would be a thing of the past and only the strong would survive.

In cities like Seattle, Minneapolis, Washington, DC, Baltimore, Philadelphia, Chicago, Los Angeles, Atlanta, Portland, and New York City, where the budgets for policing and the support for the police had been significantly diminished, crime spiked and many of those places are now scrambling to restore funding and order. The statistics are readily available on all of those cities, so I won't regurgitate them here, but it doesn't require a great deal of intellectual energy to recognize that law and order are important components of a civilized society.

Also, police officers who are respected are far less likely to react violently in tense situations. It was heartbreaking to see teenagers in New York City throwing water and other things on police officers who were simply doing their jobs. It would have been nice if those officers had had non-lethal weapons with which to protect themselves, other than Tasers. But even better than that would have been public officials and media that shamed those young people for those irrational acts of hatred that only create divisiveness in our society. Not speaking out forcefully against this foolish behavior only encourages more of it. Public officials and the media must be willing to do their part when it comes to creating harmony in our communities across the nation. If the bad actors know that city officials are not on their side, they will be much more reluctant to risk punishment for their deeds. Also, if these young criminals can be encouraged to put themselves in the shoes of those officers, they might begin to recognize the incredible danger that police officers face every day. They might also begin to realize that these individuals are human beings just like they are—they have families that are constantly worried about the safety of their beloved family member whom you may have just unnecessarily assaulted.

After the George Floyd incident, there were hundreds of riots across the country, causing more than $2 billion of damage[2] and resulting in dozens of fatalities. If the people were so concerned about George Floyd, why were they looting and destroying local businesses, many of which were owned by minority community members who had worked their entire lives to become business owners? Could it be that these rioters and looters had little concern about Mr. Floyd and were just waiting for an excuse to rob others in order to obtain something that they desired but were unwilling to work for? Many of the rioters around the country adorned themselves with Antifa or Black Lives Matter attire and boldly pursued their agendas of looting and destroying in front of iPhones and video cameras. Many of them appeared to have no concern about being arrested or prosecuted.

Unfortunately, in many of the cities that were victimized, the leadership was more interested in defunding the police than they were in prosecuting the looters. This will continue to be a problem until "the people" remove irresponsible leaders from office and install officeholders who actually care about the safety of their citizens and the property that has been earned with much hard labor. I understand that many of the looters felt aggrieved by what they perceived to be a systemically racist society and they felt justified in taking what they want as a means of adjudicating their grievances. If everyone followed their example, we would quickly devolve into absolute chaos. Therefore, these criminals should be prosecuted and at least required to make amends for what they did.

In the Black community, when children come of age,

they receive in many cases something known as "the talk." This is a conversation about how to stay alive as a Black person in a society that may not value your life. The media is always anxious to hear from some mother in that community who proclaims great fear about the safety of her children, because there are police officers out there waiting for an opportunity to beat or kill them. Many members of the progressive media talk glowingly about the responsible adults who give the talk to preserve the lives of innocent young people.

I have three sons, all of whom are Black and none of whom have ever been in trouble with the police or even had a bad racial experience with an officer. We didn't give them the talk, but we did teach them to respect the police and to obey the law. What a novel idea. My mother taught my brother and me to respect the police also, and neither of us ever had an untoward experience with the police either. I realize that by my failing to demonize the police, some will see me as a race traitor or worse, but as a follower of Jesus Christ, I feel obligated to stick with the truth regardless of the consequences.

In the cities that wish to defund the police, many of the advocates of such a policy want to substitute trained social workers who they feel can defuse situations without the use of force. I suspect that many of the bureaucrats suggesting such an idea have not witnessed the tense situations that frequently arise at the sites of domestic violence. Often the involved individuals are inebriated or high on drugs and reasoning with them just is not possible. They sometimes see the intervener as an enemy who needs to be destroyed and they violently attack. Sometimes that attack ends with a police officer shooting and killing the attacker. This is another situation where alternative nonlethal methods of restraint could prove invaluable.

I cannot think of a situation where a potentially dangerous attacker should be confronted by a social worker alone. This puts the social worker at risk. Having the social worker accompanied by a police officer could potentially be useful, or it could just add another person to the complex mix and provide yet another target for the culprit. This does not mean that the idea should be completely abandoned, but more thorough studies need to be done in terms of how the implementation of such a program should be handled. Also, we should recognize that if the police are defunded, there may not be extra bodies available to accompany the social workers.

The George Floyd incident lit a powder keg of pent-up frustrations, but it also provided an excuse for many with criminal intent to fulfill their selfish desires. From this discussion it is clear that there are areas involving policing that could benefit from some well-thought-out reforms, including how to acquire and use nonlethal methods of restraint. To achieve success, it will be necessary for the entire legal system to work together. Having a city prosecutor who is pro-criminal when everyone else is working hard to restore or maintain order doesn't work. Putting the interest of citizens on the front burner will make a big difference. That also entails looking for ways to discourage criminal activity on behalf of the community and looking for ways to reintroduce, in a successful way, prison inmates who are being released. If we truly care about all these individuals, instead of looking to score political points, we can solve these problems.

CHAPTER 7

Media and Big Tech

IF A TREE FALLS IN THE forest and there is no one around to hear it, does it make a sound? This famous question has challenged philosophers for a very long time. We will not delve into the answer here, but we will ask an analogous question. If a former president has a lot to say but social media and big tech shut him down, is he being silenced? I don't expect you to answer that question but rather to think about the incredible power given to social media and big tech, to the extent that they can essentially silence a powerful figure like the former president of the United States.

One of the most precious freedoms that we enjoy in America is freedom of speech. It is guaranteed in the First Amendment to the Constitution of the United States. Our founders really cherished the ability to speak your mind, because some of them had been born in places where challenging the ruling authorities could result in many punitive measures, up to and including the loss of your head. In America one of the real champions of free speech has been the media. In fact, there is only one business that is protected by the U.S. Constitution, and that is the press. Our country was supposed to be guided by the will of the people. Obviously, the will of the people is informed by the events occurring around them. The people were to be made aware of those events and what they meant by a free press. The word "free" is particularly important in that sentence, because in Europe and in many other places the press was frequently controlled to a large extent by the state. That free press can rapidly inform the people about infractions on their freedom by political leaders. Without the press and media in general, the people might never know about such things and might therefore blindly comply with rules and directives issued by the ruling class.

Many people rightly praise the media for helping to improve the atmosphere around many social issues over the course of time. Some people say that because we have such an active press and social media, it is unlikely that we will ever see the loss of basic freedoms such as speech. Unfortunately, that is not true. The government is not the only entity capable of suppressing speech in our country. Significant suppression of speech started with political correctness and has progressed to the "woke" movement.

When social media and the press combine to punish people who do or say the "wrong" things according to their gospel, and they punish these people with cancellation, job loss, damaged reputation, or a host of other things, with the complicity of the government, this is nothing short of restriction of speech and is antithetical to the First Amendment of the Constitution. The fact that America has so easily slipped into a position where its citizens are reluctant to express their opinions in public is cause for great alarm. Our media will play a very large role in determining whether we remain a free nation.

Media can be a powerful influence on societal thinking. A good early example of this was the release of the classic movie *The Birth of a Nation*. This 1915 film was three hours long and was quite controversial from the beginning. It was about the relationship between two families, one in the North and one in the South, during the time of conflict between the two regions. Blacks in the film were depicted as bumbling, oversexed idiots and the Ku Klux Klan were depicted as the saviors of sanity and white supremacy. While Blacks protested the film, whites flocked to the cinema in record numbers, making it highly successful. The real impact, however, was on the way it helped revive the dying Ku Klux Klan. Shamefully, the movie was even shown at the White House for the enjoyment of President Woodrow Wilson, his family, and cabinet members. Lending that kind of credibility to racist propaganda cloaked in the mantle of entertainment was very deleterious to already delicate racial relationships in America. Much of the racism that existed in America at that time was secondary to the false impression that Black people were more closely related to apes than to white people. Segregation was essential to ensure that white people did not get a chance to really know Black people, in which case they would have seen quite clearly that they were normal human beings like anyone else.

The media did not stop its malicious spread of rumors with *The Birth of a Nation*, but continued its soft bigotry with negative portrayals of Black children in shows like *The Little Rascals* and movies like *Tarzan of the Apes* in which the white man was extremely wise and powerful while the Black natives were generally much less capable, to put it mildly. As generation after generation of Americans grew up seeing negative portrayals of Blacks and very powerful and inspiring portrayals of whites, is it any wonder that racist attitudes were cultivated?

When I was growing up, I vividly remember how excited everyone would be whenever a Black person was on television in a non-servile role. It was a rare occurrence in the 1950s and early to mid-1960s, but in the late 1960s Hollywood started realizing that it could play a positive role in the civil rights movement by helping to change the image of Black Americans. Some of the first shows to emerge with leading Black characters were *I Spy*, costarring Bill Cosby, and *Julia*, starring Diahann Carroll. In the *I Spy* series, Bill Cosby and Robert Culp were international espionage agents who were extremely clever and always outsmarted their adversaries. This really broke new ground on television since it depicted a Black person as being smart and ethical. Do keep in mind that we're talking about acting. In the case of *Julia*, Diahann Carroll played the role of a professional nurse who was extremely competent and wise as she juggled her career with raising her son without a father. Her employer was a white man who was extremely kind to her, setting an example for white America about how they should treat their fellow citizens who happen to be Black. These two shows were quite popular and paved the way for a host of other series featuring Black actors in positive roles. Attitudes throughout the nation began to change quickly, demonstrating the enormous power wielded by the media.

A demographic group treated just as poorly as the Blacks early on were the American Indians. Although there were a few positive images, such as Tonto, the sidekick of the Lone Ranger, and Hawkeye's friend Chingachgook, the last of the Mohicans, the vast majority of Indians on television were portrayed as savages who wantonly murdered white people and took their scalps. Dehumanizing Indians made it easy to keep them sequestered on reservations. Fortunately, even though drug use and alcoholism remain a significant problem on reservations, the federal government has been able to enact some beneficial policies to help Native Americans integrate themselves more into the general population while maintaining their cultural heritage. Importantly, the media is now careful to portray Indians quite differently, which is helpful overall.

The portrayal of Asians by the media has been all over the place. Sometimes they are seen as gracious and kind people and at other times as scheming and dishonest. Currently the more left-leaning media do not seem to be sure whether they should be cozying up to China or condemning that nation's divisive tactics and tendency to pilfer technology. Their decision will be important as tensions escalate between the United States and China.

Perhaps one of the most noble contributions of the media to civilization was their advocacy of equal rights during the civil rights movement in America. News cameramen often embedded themselves with the civil rights protesters and in many cases even suffered physically at the hands of southern law enforcement personnel, who were not eager to have their brutality displayed for the whole world to see. Obviously, the abuses against Black people in the South had been going on for a long time. But the national conscience awakened only after the media began repeatedly displaying the unwarranted violence against Black protesters and shared stories of hate-filled white southerners persecuting Blacks.

It's not so much that people didn't know that Blacks were being treated unfairly in the South. It was the comfort of ignorance about the details of that unfairness that was disturbed by the media-led visualization every night on the national news. Racism became a national topic of interest because of the media. And suddenly there were Freedom Riders and a plethora of civic-oriented nonprofit groups focusing their attention on the atrocities going on in our nation.

There were specials on television about the civil rights movement, and there was much coverage of the fact that the movement's leader, Dr. Martin Luther King Jr., received the Nobel Peace Prize. Whenever he was imprisoned for peacefully protesting, the media was ubiquitous, proclaiming from the rooftops the injustice of the situation. This brought even more support, both emotional and financial, which helped promote one of the biggest social revolutions in the history of mankind. This was perhaps the crowning moment of media-driven righteousness.

Following this tremendous victory, the media began to focus their attention on the war in Vietnam. Having experienced the glorious fruit of media-driven positive social change, the media found their courage markedly enhanced. Not only did they cover the war, but many correspondents embedded themselves with troops in very dangerous situations. Some journalists were captured or killed by Vietcong warriors. There was also very heavy coverage of the protests on college campuses and in the streets. The media constantly fanned the flames of discord with respect to the war, ultimately changing the narrative to one in which we were the bad guys and should leave. As more Americans grew weary of the war, the media began to campaign actively against it. Some members of the media who had not previously been particularly fond of Muhammad Ali began to write favorably about him because of his opposition to the war and his courage to defy government orders.

The power of the media, and especially the internet, was not always used for good. There was a time when young people were not exposed to explicit sexual material unless they were able to surreptitiously acquire a *Playboy* magazine (at which time the possessor suddenly became quite popular). With the advent of the internet, X-rated sexual material became readily available to young people who were trying to develop their sense of identity. This is an area where big tech decided to chase the almighty dollar rather than pursue the healthy development of our young people. Between the displays of promiscuity on television and on the internet, sexual mores greatly weakened and sexually transmitted diseases skyrocketed.

One of the sexually transmitted diseases that initially was a death sentence was AIDS. In the beginning, this appeared to be confined to the gay community. Gay pride had been given birth and the media took up their banner and became a very vocal advocate for normalization of homosexual activity and status. The general public still viewed homosexuality as something that was abnormal, but the media was determined to make it fully normal and acceptable in a tolerant society. As a result of that advocacy, there is no longer a need for a closet existence for homosexuals. The media has also seized upon the cause of transsexual individuals. They are now determined to normalize this behavior as well.

This may be one of the reasons why the media has become hostile to the church and to Christianity. The Bible condemns homosexuality in both the Old and New Testaments. However, the Bible also makes it clear that God does not hate sinners, only the sin, and that Jesus died for everyone, including homosexuals.

The point is, by constantly advocating a point of view, the media and big tech can shape the definitions of morality and appropriate behavior. They have the ability to declare which people are compassionate and understand important social issues (the "woke"), and which people should be despised and/or canceled because they are hateful, intolerant, and dangerous to a well-functioning society. This is a massive amount of power to place in the hands of individuals who are unelected and do not have to answer to anyone. The likelihood that such power would not be abused is very small.

This is the reason why our founders put so much emphasis on freedom of speech, freedom of thought, and freedom of expression. They felt that tyranny would never find a home on our shores as long as the press and the people could freely resist the planting of its seeds. When the media do not resist the imposition of penalties for expressing certain points of view, or, even worse, facilitate the suppression of adversarial viewpoints, the doors leading to tyranny have been unlocked. Tyranny frequently begins with the scapegoating of any segment of the population that does not agree with the prescribed agenda of those in power.

At first, with the complicity of the press and social media, the targeted group is humiliated and demonized as the ones responsible for some undesirable event or situation that is causing distress for everyone. Next, fines or penalties or restrictions are placed on the group, making it difficult for them to provide for themselves or their families. Finally, they are imprisoned or eliminated. This is a well-established pattern that is proven by historical analysis of civilizations that have adopted socialism and subsequently communism. All of this is to provide insight into the enormous influence that the media and big tech have acquired. It can be used for good or for evil. In America we cannot put our heads in the sand and hope for the best. Significant intellectual energy must be devoted to stemming the tide of tyranny before it is too late.

One might think that I am anti-media and anti–big tech. That is not true, but I am opposed to those entities using their substantial power in a biased and domineering manner. As I stated earlier, even though they have a mixed history of both good and evil accomplishments, until recently on balance they have accomplished good things. It is unlikely that the civil rights movement of the 1960s and '70s could have been successful without the media's enthusiastic involvement, and I am very grateful for that participation.

However, there is concern about big-picture issues like overall societal success, which will be limited for young people who have been indoctrinated to believe that they are victims and are unlikely to achieve at the same level as someone who is privileged in our society. By advocating for critical race theory and other divisive philosophical viewpoints, the media are undoing so much of their previous good works. We must all realize that this is America, the place where the "can do" spirit has flourished in the past. This is the reason why people risk arrest, rape, murder, and physical abuse to get to this country and participate in the American dream. By constantly harping on negative stories and minimizing the inspirational ones, the media are causing great harm, and unfortunately most of them simply don't realize it and see themselves as saviors.

I have personally experienced both sides of the media. Before they knew I held conservative views and before I became a member of the Trump administration, I was a media darling who was held up as an example of the American dream accomplished. *Time* magazine and CNN named me as one of the twenty foremost physicians and scientists in the United States. I was awarded the Spingarn Medal, which is the highest annual award given out by the NAACP. I received the Ralph Metcalfe Award for Health from the Congressional Black Caucus Foundation. I received more than seventy honorary doctorate degrees. And the list goes on and on for years—until it abruptly stopped, because I fell out of favor with many of the powers that be and, importantly, many who control the media. This does not upset me, because I only need to do those things that leave me in the favor of God. The amount of time we spend on this earth is a drop in the bucket against the backdrop of eternity.

Nevertheless, my own personal example is proof positive of how the media is able to impact the lives of individual citizens. This makes the media very formidable, and it causes many people to cower in the corner, hoping not to be noticed, rather than boldly proclaim their beliefs. It must, however, be remembered that freedom is not free. We must be willing to fight for it each and every day, even if there is a cost associated with that fight, because the rewards of freedom greatly exceed those of comfort.

There was a time when today's media would have provoked significant conflict with the Black community, because the latter group was once very much invested in religion and a relationship with God. As the Black community has moved further away from its past strong ties to the church, the media has felt emboldened to attack and diminish religion and those who outwardly profess a strong relationship with God. Many in the progressive movement, which is of course closely aligned with social media and big tech, are hostile to many of the concepts expressed by those whose beliefs are rooted in the Bible. The Bible condemns not only homosexuality, but a whole host of sexual activities that occur outside of marriage. The murder of unborn babies is also antithetical to biblical teachings, again creating a great deal of conflict between the church and modern media. Significant effort is invested in maintaining a semblance of solidarity between the

Black community and the progressive left and its obedient media. That solidarity could be threatened if there are overt attacks on the Bible and its principles. Thus there is currently a kind of truce between the groups and an uncomfortable silence about their conflicting views.

Today, social media and big tech have set their sights on several targets, one of which is interracial relationships and marriage. A host of movies featuring interracial couples has appeared recently, and commercials on television are exploding with happily married or involved interracial couples. At first it was white men with Black women, which seemed to cause the least amount of anxiety. Now our society seems to be comfortable with the idea of Black men marrying or dating white women, and this is reflected in all kinds of ads for all kinds of products. It's interesting that this, which is one of the last barriers to full social integration, is moving along rapidly while at the same time many progressives are proclaiming that everything about our nation is based on racism. As they say, that does not compute.

Maybe the media will at some point realize that we have made tremendous racial progress here in America in just my lifetime. Not only was a Black man elected twice as president, but Black CEOs and presidents of universities and other organizations are now commonplace. The Black middle class has significantly expanded and there are now many Black millionaires and a few billionaires. Significant progress still needs to be made, but that might go faster if we highlighted the progress rather than the mistakes. It is perfectly okay to talk about slavery, Jim Crow, segregation, and general racism, but those are not the foundation of our country and are not the things that made America great. Our unity is what makes us strong, and a media that realizes that would certainly be timely right now. I realize it is very unlikely that social media and big tech will understand what a healing balm they could be, but we can hope and pray for a new cadre of young journalists who love what America stands for and are courageous enough to buck the system and tell the truth about all the issues facing us.

It's interesting to watch how the progressive media have embraced the ideas and principles of socialism and communism while eschewing the foundational pillars of a very successful capitalist society that has provided a higher standard of living for millions of people than any other system in the world. The press has been able to maneuver easily and freely in this environment. Perhaps what many of them fail to realize is that one of the first things that occurs in a socialist or communist regime is suppression of free speech and complete control of the press and all mechanisms of communication. One would not have to be a professional researcher to quickly uncover the truth of that statement. This means that by pursuing a course in which the press becomes the mouthpiece for a particular party, they are sowing the seeds of their own demise without realizing it. Black people in America have traditionally been truth seekers and I suspect that they will eventually recognize who has their best interest in mind and who is simply using them for the purpose of gaining political power that will allow them to change America into something that will not be recognizable. Will the media align themselves with the truth seekers or will they find it more convenient to stick with the power structure and do its bidding?

Interestingly, as most of the media went charging off into the progressive camp, a new media power emerged: the Fox News Channel. Instead of just promoting one point of view, Fox tried to be fair and balanced and provided plenty of airtime for views on both sides of a given issue. They were castigated by many in the mainstream media for not toeing the line and being in lockstep with their colleagues in the news business. This nontraditional approach yielded great rewards in the battles for viewership and ratings. More important, it paved the way for other outlets that had something other than a progressive ideology in the driver's seat. Some progressive politicians openly called for the disenfranchisement of the Fox News Channel. There are still many politicians today, particularly on the progressive side, who are adamantly opposed to fair and balanced reporting and instead want only their point of view put forth. When the media complies with their wishes, it becomes a political tool rather than an ally of the people.

Rather than waiting for the traditional media to see

the light and accept their role as champions of free speech, some new social media platforms are coming forth that promise to allow all points of view to be heard without censorship of anything other than child pornography. This may be the best news we have heard in a very long time, because the alternative is to break up the arguably monopolistic big tech companies, which in a way is antagonistic to the concept of free enterprise and capitalism, not to mention freedom of expression. It is clearly preferable to encourage and facilitate the development of competitors than to forcefully control legal behavior. When, however, monopolies are present and have reached a point where virtually everyone has to use them, there may be a role for some governmental regulation to ensure fairness and equal distribution of services.

It is easy to see from this discussion that in a free society where capitalism reigns, abusive and dominating behavior can readily emerge if the watchdogs of the society are not attentive or are distracted. The watchdogs are the media, and things can deteriorate even more rapidly when they join with the perpetrators of abuse and domination to attempt control of society. For over a decade now I have been vociferously warning people about the dangers of political correctness. I very much believe in being kind to people and not trying to offend people. I believe this is our Christian duty, but PC is more about controlling speech and behavior than it is about being kind to others.

It's interesting that with their allies in pop culture, the

media get to decide what is offensive and what is not offensive to whom. Why should any of us give someone else the power to determine what offends us? If I wanted to destroy a peaceful society, I would certainly sow seeds of discord by convincing certain segments of that society that other segments were doing and saying hurtful things. By creating an atmosphere of extreme sensitivity to so many things that are said, one can distract people from concentrating on and solving the real problems. Many people in our society today have been convinced that being politically correct and "woke" places you at the pinnacle of compassion. What it really does is distract you and make you concentrate on many things that have limited meaning, at the expense of much bigger issues. For instance, if you're only concentrating on finding the right channel on the radio in your car, you might not notice that the car is heading off a cliff.

In addition to trying to always be politically correct, we have now moved away from the Judeo-Christian value system that taught us not only to tolerate our neighbors but to love them. Instead, today's progressive culture teaches us to resent any neighbor whose political views are at variance with ours and that it is perfectly permissible to hurt that person or their family. That is what cancel culture is all about. It is utterly antithetical to the spirit of community that helped our nation develop so rapidly and thrive on the world stage.

Interestingly, there is a real dilemma awaiting the

media and the advocates of cancel culture with regard to the Black community. A large number of Black Americans are skeptical about the benefits of the COVID vaccines and have refused to take them. Trying to force the issue only solidifies the resolve to resist. Historically, Americans of color have been exposed to many medical misadventures that were purposely thrust upon them, making their reluctance understandable. When you throw into the mix the repeated reversals in recommendations and the nonscientific approach, which includes things like denying the efficacy of natural immunity, it is not hard to see how skepticism might arise.

The media and big tech have not quite figured out how to approach this dilemma, but we can always hope and pray that they will want to do the right thing and help not only the Black community but all communities get the answers that they need to restore confidence in the Centers for Disease Control and other parts of the government. They can begin by asking our government to explain why so many recent studies have demonstrated that the immunity one gains after having contracted the COVID virus is vastly superior to that gained from the vaccines—yet people who have antibodies from having had the disease still must take the vaccine in order to get a vaccine passport. This obviously makes no medical sense whatsoever, but it would be good to get an explanation that can be examined. That used to be something that the media would be salivating to do, but now they take a laissez-faire attitude when there is so much at stake. If they really want to help the Black community, they should get to the bottom of the inconsistencies. This would be doing a tremendous service not only for the Black community but for America and the world.

The progressive media have also failed the Black community when it comes to the border crisis. Under the previous administration, we had the best border control ever. We also had the lowest unemployment numbers for Black Americans ever. It is no coincidence that these two never-before-seen occurrences happened simultaneously. Because the flow of illegal immigrants was down to a trickle, the jobs that many of them were filling became available to low-skilled American workers. Some conservative outlets highlighted this correlation, but most progressive outlets seldom mentioned it, if ever. If the progressive media were truly interested in the long-term circumstances of Black Americans, they would have eagerly investigated the reasons for the new prosperity and would have been looking for ways to enhance it rather than ignore it.

We can see that the media and big tech are extraordinarily powerful entities, perhaps even more influential than the federal government itself. That power can be used for good or for evil. In the past, much of that influence has been used to promote social justice, such as during the civil rights movement. Much more can be done in a positive way to complete the job. If more people enter occupations in media and big tech who love America and their fellow Americans and want to facilitate the achievement of a fair society for all, we will have a very good chance of moving in the direction of both peace and strength.

We also must concentrate on bringing a sense of morality back to America. In his two-volume analysis of early America's extraordinary success, *Democracy in America*, published in 1835 and 1840, the Frenchman Alexis de Tocqueville talked about our remarkable businesses and industries, our superior educational system, our novel and effective tripartite government, and our amazing cities, among other things. But what impressed him the most was the fiery sermons that emanated from the nation's pulpits. It was those sermons that gave a bunch of ragtag militiamen the courage and fortitude to defeat the most powerful empire on the face of the earth. Those sermons also taught people to be kind to each other and to amalgamate their strengths and talents into a powerful instrument of peace. Tocqueville concluded by saying that he wanted to know what made America great in such a short period of time, and I believe his conclusions were correct. He said America is great because America is good, and if America ever ceases to be good, she will cease to be great.

CHAPTER 8

Does Systemic Racism Exist in America?

RECENTLY THERE HAS BEEN A GREAT deal of talk about racism, but not just any racism—systemic racism. This implies that our whole social system is undergirded by racist principles, such as creating laws and policies that favor white people at the expense of minorities. It also means that all the institutions and policies that spring forth from that society are inherently racist. Even when there is no overt appearance of racially biased activity, there are some who want us to believe that racism is embedded automatically in everything that is American and that it cannot be escaped. This is very interesting given that Black people in America have made so much progress in recent decades.

By proposing that our whole social system is infected with racism at every level, the progressive left does not have to prove that specific incidents are the result of racism and can simply paint any situation with a broad brush.

I will readily admit that there are still vestiges of racism in our society, but as a Black man living every day in America, I rarely feel persecuted or disadvantaged unless I am dealing with members of the progressive left. These individuals seem to feel entitled to be able to determine what a Black person in America should think and what philosophies they should adopt. In fact, they seem to feel that they have a responsibility to single out and persecute Black people who do not abide by their definition of being Black. President Biden went so far as to say that if voters were having difficulty deciding between him and President Trump, "you ain't Black." This self-designated position as overlords of Black behavior is very offensive to many Blacks who take pride in thinking for themselves and not simply parroting what their rulers put forth.

It is critical to the goals of the progressive left to remain in a position that allows them to dictate to individuals, who in many cases are more concerned with day-to-day living than with crafting a political philosophy to govern their actions. The left discovered decades ago that by parceling out government benefits bit by bit, they could gain control of the voting habits of these individuals and create a significant political power base, especially in areas of concentrated minority neighborhoods. They are hoping to expand and solidify that power base by making it easy for many poor people to enter our country and obtain benefits provided to them through the efforts of the progressive legislators in both houses of Congress. These power-hungry politicians have the mainstream media at their beck and call to glorify and widely broadcast their efforts. At the same time, they emphasize how much money is in the hands of wealthy individuals and how that money needs to be redistributed in order to provide a more comfortable existence not only for those who are illegally immigrating to the country, but for the many American citizens who are not wealthy.

In other words, socialism is being placed front and center on the stage of American history. As in other locations, it sounds good, because the poor and needy are being taken care of, but the devil is in the details. There are never enough rich people from whom to forcefully acquire resources to provide a comfortable lifestyle for everyone. As Margaret Thatcher put it, "Socialism is great until you run out of other people's money."

Many readers are probably already seeing where I am going with this. If Black Americans can be made to feel like victims because they live in a systemically racist society that was initiated by the slave trade, it will be easy to obtain their support for socialistic redistribution of wealth in the form of reparations or just a lot of free stuff paid for by the wealthy. Creating the desire for multitudinous goods and services that are paid for by someone else is not a difficult task. Fulfilling the promise, however, is another story altogether. Obviously, those who supported these kinds of measures one time might not be willing to do so a second time if the promises are not fulfilled. The progressive left knows that, but they also know that if they can acquire enough power to completely change the political system, there won't be a next time that's analogous to the current time. By changing the power structure in such a way that they maintain power forever regardless of what voters think, they will have created something that the United States of America was never intended to be.

The original intent for our nation was to be a place where people were free to pursue whatever occupations and careers they wanted and to work as hard or as little as they wanted to. People would not have to suffer constant governmental interference in the management of their lives. If they did well financially, so be it. And if they did poorly financially, so be it. If in their private capacities they wanted to help each other, they were welcome to do so and communities could be organized in ways that suited them. All of that is turned upside down with socialism, where the government controls everything, including what you should say and think.

As the transition from free society to government-controlled society is taking place, it is useful for the government to select a social issue like racism in order to appear righteous and above the fray. Who could possibly be against enacting policies to fight racism? If racism is in everything, it provides a mechanism to impose draconian rules and policies upon the unsuspecting populace without being challenged. If there are challenges, the complicit media will not cover them or will demonize them.

From the discussion so far, it is easy to understand why it is so important for progressives to label American society as systemically racist. They must create dissatisfaction with the system that we have in order to generate enough support to change it into something else. The supposition is that whatever it changes into will not be as bad as systemic racism. This argument, of course, fails to consider the fact that America remains the dream destination for people across the globe for a reason. It also fails to take into consideration that there are many people like myself in America who came from disadvantaged backgrounds and managed to be very successful in their career choices and in wealth accumulation. Many of these individuals have gone on to dedicate their lives to improving the lives of others around them.

It is my hope and prayer that the Black community in America will soon begin to ask questions like "Are we better off in cities that are run by left-leaning progressives? Do we have better schools and higher achievement in such communities? Is there less crime in such communities? Is there a higher rate of family formation in such communities?" The list of questions could go on for quite some time, and unfortunately in almost all instances the answer is going to be no. Even though many large cities with large minority populations have had progressive mayors and city councils, which in many cases are composed of members who belong to minority groups, the charges of police brutality and other signs of racism still persist. In many large cities the power structure has been controlled by minorities for several decades with no changes in the complaints about racism. In fact, the charges seem to be increasing, but according to the proponents of all the critical theories, it doesn't matter who's in charge, because racism is built into the system and cannot be extracted. The only solution as far as they are concerned is to fundamentally change the system.

There was a time in America when systemic racism was rampant. In the late nineteenth and early twentieth centuries, Jim Crow laws were prevalent throughout the South as well as in some other parts of the country. These were local laws designed to maintain racial segregation. They were also designed to maintain white supremacy, although no one wanted to admit that.

Lawfully enforced racial segregation was officially embraced by the U.S. government when the Supreme Court accepted the case of *Plessy v. Ferguson* in 1896 and sustained the lower court ruling that essentially approved racial segregation as long as equal facilities were provided for each race. This basically established the "separate but equal" policies that reigned supreme until the mid-1960s, which was far too long. The *Plessy* ruling was never officially overruled, but it has unofficially been relegated to the dustbin of history. In 1954 the Supreme Court dealt it a death blow with the *Brown v. Board of Education* ruling that essentially outlawed segregated public education. By forcefully stating that all American citizens are to be treated equally under the law, this ruling began the unraveling of one of the fundamental pillars of systemic racism.

It is very appropriate that the battle for equal rights should begin with the educational system. Education can provide anyone from any circumstance with a tremendous advantage when it comes to climbing the ladder of opportunity in this nation. This is the reason why during slavery it was illegal to teach slaves to read. By keeping a group ignorant, it becomes much easier to control them. Even today, the progressive media and big tech understand the principle of ignorance and control. They purposefully suppress information and stories about things that are not consistent with the narratives they put forth. At the same time, they widely broadcast stories about incidents that fortify their arguments. If, for instance, there is a case of a white police officer killing an unarmed Black man, everyone will know about that case, including the names of all the involved individuals. That kind of case fits the narrative of systemic police racial bias. The reports that accompany such a story seldom indicate how rare such incidents are today, but instead try to imply that they are daily occurrences. Statistical records make it quite clear that there is no epidemic of police shootings of Black people in America.[1]

Even though it is difficult to achieve consensus on exactly how many Black men are killed by police every year and how many police are killed by Black men, there is general agreement that approximately one thousand people are killed by police in America each year.[2] Every one of those deaths is a tragedy. However, since there are between fifty-five and sixty million encounters between citizens and police annually, the rate of fatal encounters is about one in every fifty-seven thousand encounters. Demographically, groups that are economically deprived and environmentally challenged tend to be involved in the kinds of activities that would invite police encounters, making it unsurprising that those groups would have disproportionately more fatal encounters. Again it should be emphasized that regardless of the cause of the fatal encounter, every one of those deaths is a tragedy and we need to strive to find ways to decrease or eliminate such incidents.

When you consider the millions of police/citizen encounters and the relatively few incidents resulting in the use of deadly police force, you have to question all the hysteria around the few cases of inappropriate police gun violence. This is not to say that it doesn't occur, but it should be clearly stated that it is not a common occurrence and does not justify the label of systemic racism.

Showing that there is no basis for the charge of systemic racism in the police departments of America is not enough. We also need to try to understand why there is so much violence in the Black community that results in an increased number of police encounters. Since more than 70 percent of Black children born in America are born to single mothers,[3] it is very possible that growing up without a role model and an authority figure could make boys vulnerable to the influences of the street, which include inappropriate violence. This is a societal problem that requires immediate significant attention. I have had an opportunity to visit many neighborhood nonprofit organizations across the country, such as HOPE Farm in Fort Worth, Texas, that concentrate on providing strong role models and helpers for boys growing up in disadvantaged situations, including single-parent homes. The transition seen in the lives of these boys is absolutely remarkable, and virtually all of these organizations welcome volunteers and donations from the community. There is no reason why we cannot all be involved in helping to solve this problem.

Returning to the issue of education, if we want to truly provide equal opportunities for all of our citizens, we need to take a serious look at how public education is funded in this country. Currently much of public education is locally funded, which means that children in affluent areas will attend schools with better-trained personnel and much better facilities and equipment than children living in less affluent areas. That will of course contribute to the achievement gap and is blatantly unfair to children who already start out in life with significant economic disadvantages. These kinds of situations are ripe for the cultivation of resentment and even hatred. Of course, some people will immediately criticize what I just said, complaining that I just served all teachers in poor school districts with an indictment of inferiority. A more intelligent reading is that I am simply acknowledging that the most attractive educational environments tend to attract the best-trained individuals. That is not to say that some of the very dedicated teaching staff in some of the disadvantaged school districts are not superb educators who deserve much admiration for their selfless devotion to others. There was a time when I would not have needed to explain that, but today we live in such a highly sensitive atmosphere that almost nothing said escapes critical analysis and the attribution of nefarious intent.

Remaining on the educational theme, the public schools I attended were all in economically deprived areas and lacked many of the facilities, programs, and opportunities that I have seen in schools located in privileged areas. However, public libraries were available at no cost and I also had access to the libraries and museums of institutions of higher learning that were in the area. By utilizing those facilities, I was able to supplement my educational exposure tremendously, which closed the educational gap between myself and children growing up in various affluent areas around Detroit. Furthermore, many of my teachers provided extra help and recommendations for me after school because they recognized the tremendous thirst I had for education.

I believe it is that same kind of drive and motivation that is responsible for the fact that there is no achievement or wealth gap in America between Nigerians and white Americans. Even though Nigerians and Ghanaians are Black, they place a premium on education and subsequently are very high achievers. Could it be that instead of teaching Black children that they are victims of a racist society, we should be emphasizing to them the importance of solid academic achievement and self-reliance?

That emphasis on academic achievement would be facilitated by a better system of financial support for schools located in economically depressed areas. It would be beneficial to our entire population in America if we could find a way and the will to properly educate all of our children. It has nothing to do with racism, but it has everything to do with whether we care. I say this because the public school systems in Appalachia and poor white districts are also seriously lacking in the elements that promote good education. This is a matter of national import, because even though we have one-quarter as many people as China or India, we will still have to compete with them on the world stage with the population that we have. That means we cannot afford to fail to develop any of our people.

It is critical that we learn to teach our children the correct history of our nation. We should not hide any aspects of our history, but we should also promote pride in some of the incredibly inspirational moments of our past. We should remember that our history provides the basis for our identity, and our identity provides the basis for our beliefs. How can we have a healthy belief system without an accurate and positive sense of who we are and where we came from?

In the past, and certainly when I was in school, there was little or no mention during American history classes of positive contributions to our nation by Black people. Yet there are few environments you could inhabit without seeing something that was invented or developed by a Black person. For instance, the light provided through that light bulb in your room was influenced by Lewis Latimer, who was the right-hand man of Thomas Edison and came up with a filament for the light bulb that lasted more than two or three days. He also invented the electric lamp and diagrammed the telephone for Alexander Graham Bell. Despite that, few people know his name. When you get in your car and come to a stop at the traffic signal, it might behoove you to know that the traffic signal was invented by Garrett Morgan, a Black man who also invented the gas mask, which saved lots of lives during the First World War. Speaking of wars, we should mention Henrietta Bradberry, a Black woman who invented the underwater cannon, making it possible to launch torpedoes from submarines. When we cross the railroad tracks, we could talk about Andrew Beard, who invented the automatic railroad car coupler, and Elijah McCoy, who invented the automatic lubrication system for locomotive engines and was such a precise inventor that people were always trying to imitate him. Purchasers would want to know if something was Elijah McCoy's innovation, hence the phrase "the real McCoy." I could go on for a long time talking about common inventions that we all use on a daily basis that were invented by Black people with no acknowledgment in our history books until very recently.

In America we have a very racially diverse population, and I could talk about tremendous contributions to our success as a nation made by each and every one of those races. You see, our diversity is not a problem, unless we make it into a problem. The fact is, the ability to look at things from many different viewpoints and solve common problems is a tremendous advantage and is perhaps one of the chief reasons why our nation ascended to the pinnacle of the world in record time. These are the kinds of lessons we need to be teaching our children. Those who are attempting to drive wedges between the different demographics that make up America are enemies of the state and should be ignored.

The purveyors of critical race theory and the 1619 Project seem to give the impression that America is uniquely racist as opposed to all the other nations throughout history that practiced slavery. Again, I cannot emphasize how horrible the practice of slavery was—and is today, when there are more slaves throughout the world than ever before.[4] I am sometimes brought to tears as I think about some of our ancestors who had to endure humiliation, torture, and unimaginable grief as family members were sold off, never to be seen again, but we must remember that these things are part and parcel of slavery and they occurred in every nation where slavery was practiced.

As I mentioned in chapter 4, it should also be noted that the vast majority of southern whites did not own slaves. Slaves were a luxury item that could only be afforded by wealthy landowners. What is unique about America is that so many of our citizens were so vehemently opposed to the institution of slavery that they gave birth to a vibrant abolitionist movement. The abolitionists helped many slaves escape to the North and to Canada and also fueled the resolve to maintain the Union, which was threatened because the South wanted to maintain the economic advantages it was afforded by slavery.

For a nation to be torn apart by a civil war in which brother was fighting against brother and unfathomable emotional pain was suffered, the issues at stake would have to be overwhelmingly important. We should be proud that our country had citizens with that level of morality and courage to be willing to sacrifice virtually everything to defeat this evil institution. That is what makes us truly unique. We should not allow anyone to twist the facts and create a narrative that can label our entire system as racist when we had so many who sacrificed so much to fight for liberty and justice for all.

If, in fact, the American system is riddled with racism, the only remedy would be to replace it with something totally new. This, I believe, is the point that many on the left are trying to make. If it is true that racism is woven into the very fabric of our nation, then it should not be possible for Blacks and other minorities to become successful in such a system. As I have previously observed, Blacks have ascended to many of the most powerful and prestigious positions in America. Many major philanthropic and nonprofit organizations are headed up by Blacks in today's America. Many of the very highest positions in government are now occupied by Blacks. Many of the decisive positions in sports and entertainment are held by Blacks. In short, in my lifetime Blacks have demonstrated that they are capable of fulfilling virtually all roles in America, and to say that we have a systemically racist system that precludes Black success is ludicrous.

The situation we find ourselves in as a nation reminds me of an older sibling who badly wants a delicious treat that the younger sibling is in possession of. The older sibling begins to tell the younger one that the treat he is eating contains dead bugs and a host of distasteful ingredients. The younger sibling becomes nauseous and puts the treat down and leaves the scene, at which time the older sibling grabs the treat and consumes it with great joy. In order to change our system of governance, which works at least as well as any other in the history of the world, the progressives must create that sense of disgust that will create in vulnerable people a desire to fundamentally change our system.

We do not need to fundamentally change our system, but we do need to continually examine it and make appropriate changes to enhance the goals of providing liberty and justice for all. Life, liberty, and the pursuit of happiness must always be front and center. We must be extremely wary of any proposals that restrict people's freedoms by canceling them or impacting their ability to make a living, travel freely, or speak their mind. Remember, historically, totalitarian governments start out by identifying a group that they can label as troublemakers, simply because that group has different opinions about how things should be done. Next, if they have the power to do so, they began to persecute that group. If we allow this to occur in our society, we will be participating in the destruction of the greatest nation in the history of the world.

It is important to remember that not all of the people who belong to the group of persecutors are necessarily bad people. They have just been indoctrinated to believe that their point of view is the only correct one and that those who disagree with them are misguided and need help to find their way. The radical jihadists think the same way.

As far as they are concerned, those who disagree with them are infidels who need to either be converted or eliminated. They believe that there is no sin in deceiving or harming the infidels and their families. We can already see the beginnings of these kinds of attitudes in America, and we cannot take a nonchalant attitude and assume that things will return to normal automatically.

Vigorously resisting the idea that all of our policies and institutions are fundamentally racist is a good starting point. We must also aggressively highlight the inconsistencies in the arguments about systemic racism in our country. For instance, how can a systemically racist country in which a significant majority of the population is white twice elect a Black president? How could such a country have had a Black chairman of the Joint Chiefs of Staff? How could it have had Black secretaries of state or a Black vice president of the United States? I could go on with these kinds of questions almost indefinitely. As a nation we simply have to think for ourselves and not let someone convince us of an alternate reality when our eyes, ears, and brain tell us something else.

My own experience as a candidate for the Republican nomination for president of the United States also sheds light on the situation. I was one of seventeen candidates and at one point during the campaign was the front-runner. I traveled extensively and encountered well-informed, enthusiastic crowds even in the smallest little hamlets in sparsely populated states. At no time did I feel hampered by the color of my skin. The crowds were composed of every demographic group, including Blacks, whites, Latinos, Asians, Middle Easterners, old people, young people, children, military personnel, law enforcement, and more. Even in the depths of Mississippi and Alabama, the crowds were large and enthusiastic.

The only real hostility I encountered came from the left-leaning media when they began to take my candidacy seriously. What I represented was the can-do attitude that allows people to go from serious deprivation to enormous success in our society. That does not fit neatly into the narrative of victimhood and systemic racism. Before that narrative became so prominent, people like me were celebrated and held up as role models for young people to emulate. There was even a movie entitled *Gifted Hands*, starring Cuba Gooding Jr., about my life. But if critical race theory and the viability of systemic racism is to be maintained, there cannot be many people of minority status who succeed, or at least it becomes necessary to paint a picture that emphasizes failure over success.

There is a difference between systemic racism and systemic sinfulness that manifests itself as hatred, racism, unfairness, selfishness, cruelty, dishonesty, covetousness, murderousness, immorality, and a host of other evils. Just as some have characterized our society as systemically racist, one could also characterize it as any of those other manifestations I just named. A sinful society will always demonstrate the things of which it is composed, but not one of those things defines it. Allowing the media and left-leaning progressives to choose the adjective with which our society is labeled is a huge mistake and should be not only resisted but actively challenged. If leftist progressives are allowed to go unchallenged and the media endlessly to repeat their charges, people begin to believe their allegations of systemic racism. They begin to accept some of the outrageous remedies proposed, which include teaching our children, if they are white, that they are oppressors, and if they are Black, that they are victims. This child abuse must stop. This is the land of opportunity for everyone and we must continue to emphasize that the person who has the most to do with what happens to you is *you*.

In medicine, the charges of racism are multitudinous and have been present for a very long time. Traditionally there is a hierarchy in patient care. Attending physicians frequently take care of private patients, while the resident staff, led by a chief resident, takes care of patients who do not have a private physician. In many of our inner cities, the private patients tend to be white and the nonprivate patients Black. This automatically makes people think that there is a two-tiered system. The same system exists, however, in Appalachia and in places where there are no or very few Blacks. I have never witnessed a situation in which the chief resident or one of the other resident staff were not able to get guidance from the attending staff when they encountered a problem with one of the non-private patients. Whether or not this is the correct system is immaterial to the point that I'm making here. That point is that some things that appear on the surface to be racially motivated are not what they appear to be. It is always a good idea to study the situation in depth before launching malicious charges that will not stand up to honest investigation.

Many progressive mayors, police chiefs, city council members, and other urban leaders attempt to excuse the total mess in their cities by saying that the carnage is a result of long-term systemic racism. Nevertheless, we have seen numerous examples of vast improvements in crime and economic development when appropriate leadership emerges. Notably, a few decades ago New York City was a bastion of crime, with skyrocketing murder rates. When Rudy Giuliani was elected mayor, he surrounded himself with people who were serious about bringing law and order back to the streets of New York. The city went from the worst city in violent crime to one of the best in a relatively short time. I'm sure there are many people who detest Giuliani because of his association with Donald Trump, whom they detest even more, but it's hard to argue with the results.

Rather than blaming everything on systemic racism, our failing cities should think about appropriate support of law enforcement with changes where necessary and major investment in solid education for all children, including those in economically deprived areas. This does not need to be about political parties so much as about the welfare of the citizens of our cities and our nation.

CHAPTER 9

Judeo-Christian Values and Racism

SOME HAVE CLAIMED THAT THE BIBLE condones slavery and the mastery of one race over another. In the ninth chapter of the book of Genesis, verses 18–27, there is a story about Noah and his sons. One of his sons, by the name of Ham, looked upon his father's nakedness while he was drunk, which was considered a cultural transgression, and he was therefore designated to be a servant to his brothers. For reasons that are unclear, some biblical scholars have concluded that Ham was Black and therefore his Black descendants were cursed to be slaves. Interestingly, the Bible says nothing about the color of Ham's skin, so this is an early example of "fake news." It is also an example of how people have tried to twist the words of the Bible in order to make them comply with their less-than-noble desires and beliefs.

What does the Bible really say about how we should treat others of different racial identities? In the tenth chapter of the New Testament book of Luke, verses 30–37, Jesus Himself answers this question. As we all know, the Bible admonishes us to love our neighbors. Jesus was asked the question, who is my neighbor? He proceeded to tell the story of the Good Samaritan. If you think the tension between Black people and white people in America is significant, it was minor compared to that between Jews and Samaritans. They wanted nothing to do with each other, and certainly would not want to be in physical contact with each other. In the story told by Jesus, a Jewish man was attacked and severely beaten by robbers and left for dead. A Jewish priest and a Jewish Levite both walked by the man on the other side of the street, failing to even ascertain his viability. A Samaritan found him and rendered aid and set him upon his donkey and took him to an inn where he paid for his upkeep and told the innkeeper that he would be returning shortly from his journey and would reimburse him for any further bills that were incurred. Jesus made it clear that the Samaritan, and not the fellow Jews, was this man's neighbor. Jesus further admonished the questioner to go and do likewise. Since Jesus was a Jew Himself, this story makes it extraordinarily clear that He felt that people are people and that they should all be treated fairly and with respect and even love.

This famous story is celebrated around the world and is commemorated in the United States by a large number of health facilities that bear the name "Good Samaritan." There are several good points made by this story, but I believe the key point is that racial differences should not alter the way we treat others. Everyone should be loved in the same way that we would like for others to love us if we were in a difficult situation. The Bible is about love and peace and a relationship with God, among other things. The messages of the Bible are intended to promote those things and not strife. When it tells slaves to be obedient to their masters (Ephesians 6:5, Colossians 3:22, 1 Peter 2:18), it is said in the context of promoting harmony, being a good example, and demonstrating the contentment that is afforded by a relationship with God. For instance, in the fifth chapter of Matthew, it says if you are struck on the cheek, to turn the other cheek, and to be kind to those who are not kind to you. This is an attitude that is not generally understood by those who do not have a relationship with a loving God.

The horrors of slavery are talked about in the Bible in several places. Notably, the children of Israel were enslaved by the Egyptians for more than four hundred years and required deliverance by God through Moses. Another famous story in the Bible is about Joseph, who was sold into slavery by his own brothers. Slavery was not portrayed as anything good, but rather as a situation that could possibly be escaped through faith in God and a diligent pursuit of excellence. It is also important to point out that in biblical times it was not unusual for someone who was in a great deal of debt or who needed money for another good reason to sell themselves into slavery for a defined period of time. In that sense, they would be more like what we see today as employees, and the biblical admonition to employees would be to be honest and to provide an excellent effort for those who hired you.

As we can see, the Bible condones neither slavery nor racism. In fact, it promotes just the opposite, which is freedom and love of one's fellow man. Those biblical admonitions helped to produce a vigorous abolitionist movement throughout the nation that contributed significantly to the end of the abominable institution of slavery. Unfortunately, the same cannot be said of racism. In fact, we have all heard it said that the eleven o'clock hour on Sunday mornings is the most segregated time in America.

I remember as a young man having some doubts about the denomination to which I belonged (Seventh-day Adventist) being a truly godly organization because throughout the country they had white conferences and Black conferences. It seemed to me that such an arrangement was not conducive to love and harmony between all of God's children. After trying many other denominations, I came back to the Adventist Church, concluding that they had the right doctrines but the wrong people. As with so many things, the founding ideas are often excellent, but the execution is lacking because it is carried out by defective individuals.

That description includes all of us, which is why we need a Savior.

Candy and I lived in Australia in the early 1980s, and in fact, our oldest son, Murray, was born there and has dual citizenship. When we returned to Maryland, it was our intention to join one of the Black Adventist churches where we knew the pastor and many members of the congregation. When we got to the church, the parking lot was overflowing and there were cars parked along the access road for a very long distance. We knew that there was a white church just three miles down the road, so we went there instead. We have now been members of that church (Spencerville SDA) for nearly forty years.

When we first started going there, Black faces were very rare, but now the church is very well integrated with a host of different nationalities, which fortunately is the case with the Seventh-day Adventist Church across the nation. Many other denominations have also seen the light and the segregated eleven o'clock hour is rapidly vanishing. Interestingly, my wife was in the choir, and early on one of the elderly white ladies came to her in private and thanked her for coming to Spencerville Church and helping her to realize that she had some racial problems that were now a thing of the past. She said she would have died and gone to hell because of those attitudes if Candy had not shown her that people are people and that Jesus loves and died for us all.

People of faith from many different denominations who

believed that mankind was created by God joined forces in Great Britain to create a significant abolitionist movement. Their influence greatly impacted efforts to end slavery in America as well. The Quakers were especially active in the fight to end slavery. Often it was fringe groups of major denominations that actually spearheaded the courageous efforts to free the slaves, because the denominational leaders lacked the courage to lead and were too concerned about their societal status. It was the belief that all men have a common ancestor and are brothers that spurred on many of the abolitionists. They believed that subjecting other members of the human family to captivity and cruelty was sinful and would result in the wrath of God being poured out upon our nation. This resulted in a sense of urgency in their mission.

Interestingly, some of the proponents of the continuation of slavery in America identified themselves as Christians, and they justified their actions by claiming that they were providing a better environment for "jungle savages" who otherwise would have no exposure to the culture of superior human beings. Furthermore, those individuals would be subjected to the terror of fierce creatures in the jungle and would be deprived of resources. In some cases, these "Christian" slave masters even created church services for the slaves and made sure that those included the passages in the Bible that encourage slaves to obey their masters. I have no doubt that some of those enslavers thought they were doing good things, but I wonder what they would have thought if they in fact had been the slaves of others. Enforced servitude is not pleasant under any circumstance, and the picture of idyllic plantations with happy slaves was another example of "fake news" meant to assuage feelings of guilt on behalf of slave owners and to dampen the opposition to slavery on behalf of northerners and others who really did not have insight into the conditions on those plantations.

Those who say that American Blacks are better off than Blacks in Africa may have some valid points, but it is only fair to point out the fact that whites in America are also generally better off than the people in the nations from which they originated. We all played a part in making America into a great nation, and we are all Americans. It is the things that unite us that make us strong, and it is the things that divide us that weaken the fabric of our nation.

I find it interesting that many of the groups in America that do not have faith-based foundations include the same people who emphasize the differences in people. For them, identity politics is almost a religion. Since they believe that we evolved from a slime pit, through a series of lesser creatures, into the intellectual beings that we have become, they also believe that there are some evolutionary differences that result in inherent differences between the races. That being the case, they claim that white people are different from Black people and that you can make judgments of people based on the external physical characteristics over which they have no control. If that kind of thinking is not racist, I'm not sure what is.

The role of the church in the abolition of slavery is perhaps the greatest example of the moral authority of the faith-based community in our country's history. However, a close second would be the role of the church in elevating the cause of the civil rights movement in the 1950s, '60s, and '70s. There was a tremendous amalgamation of Protestant Christians, Jews, Catholics, and others who put themselves in personal peril to support the struggle for equality of all Americans. Many of the protests were organized in churches by courageous leaders and community activists who often ended up behind bars or in hospitals as a result of their confrontations with local legal authorities who were upholding real systemic racism in legitimate governmental organizations.

The greatest civil rights leader in our country's history, Dr. Martin Luther King Jr., rose to prominence through his role as a minister of the gospel. His advocacy of nonviolent resistance to the evil suppression of human rights gained worldwide attention and praise as well as unprecedented support. By adhering to biblical principles, Dr. King was able to expose the evil of the then ubiquitous systemic racism that permeated American society. To claim that our society is still systemically racist is to deny the efficacy of that heroic movement and the sacrifice of millions of brave Americans who stood up for freedom and justice for all.

We briefly touched upon the subject of the "morality of

slavery" in regard to its ability to leave people in a better position than they were in when they were free. Adopting such a belief system obviously requires a strong sense of rationalization. Nevertheless, today we have political philosophies that approach governing with the same rationalization. Adherents of these philosophies feel that they know what is best for others and, because they have political power, that they should impose their will upon people who sometimes don't understand that it is for their own good. This is nothing new or unique to America. In fact, this is the philosophy that reigned supreme in nations that were ruled by monarchs who supposedly possessed superior insight into what was good for all the people. This certainly is the philosophy held by Marxist rulers and communist/socialist regimes. This kind of thinking is antithetical to the founding principles of our great nation, which was supposed to be governed with respect to the will of the people. That made America into a very different place that was considered a great experiment on the world stage. That experiment is ongoing, and it is yet to be determined whether a nation can rise and be sustained on the will of the people or must indeed have a dominant governing structure that overrules the will of the people and imposes its own, which it claims is more beneficial.

One of the reasons why America has remained a free nation and maintained life, liberty, and the pursuit of happiness as God-given rights is because of the revered position of churches and our faith-based communities. If the position of faith-based communities is diminished and freedom of religion is compromised by the government, all of our other freedoms will also be compromised. This is the reason that the very first amendment to the Constitution of the United States of America emphasizes freedom of religion. That amendment reads as follows:

> Congress shall make no law respecting an establishment of religion, or prohibiting the free exercise thereof; or abridging the freedom of speech, or of the press; or the right of the people peaceably to assemble, and to petition the Government for a redress of grievances.

The first part of the amendment stems from the fact that many of the people involved in the writing of our Constitution came from nations that suffered significant violence and destruction at the hands of religious zealots who controlled the government. They wanted to make sure that we did not provide an avenue to allow the creation of a theocracy in America. This should be understandable to everyone, and we should all be thankful for this language.

The second part of the sentence, "or prohibiting the free exercise thereof," is frequently glossed over without much consideration. It simply means that a person in our society should not have to hide their religious beliefs and should be able to live according to those beliefs without penalty.

Many religious beliefs in our country are biblically based. There is the well-known case of Jack Phillips, who owns a cake shop and was sued by a homosexual couple because he refused to bake a wedding cake that promoted a homosexual theme. He said that refusal was based on his biblical belief that homosexuality is an abomination to God. Without question, there are some forceful and difficult-to-misinterpret passages in the Bible opposing homosexual activity. Strongly held religious beliefs based on those passages that inform one's actions should be protected if religious liberty is indeed one of our foundational convictions. Jack Phillips, as an American citizen, has the right to produce the kinds of products he believes in. There is no right provided in our founding documents to force people to produce products they oppose. Our free market economy allows their business to flourish or fail based on their ability to produce products that are desired by the population they serve. When we begin to tell free Americans what they can and cannot produce, they are no longer free, and this must be resisted. The case went all the way to the Supreme Court and Phillips won.

However, it is vitally important that we remember that discrimination is illegal and we must expend significant effort to distinguish between legitimate religious beliefs and the use of religion to excuse discrimination. There were southern slave owners who tried to justify slavery through distortion or out-of-context utilization of biblical texts. Of course, admonitions against bondage and servitude are found throughout the scriptures, and when the Bible is contextually read, there can be no question about which side of the slavery argument it supports. For example, Proverbs 24:11–12 says, "If thou forbear to deliver them that are drawn unto death, and those that are ready to be slain; if thou sayest, Behold, we knew it not; doth not he that pondereth the heart consider it? and he that keepeth thy soul, doth not he know it? and shall not he render to every man according to his works?" This passage, written by the wisest man who ever lived, tells people of faith that they have an obligation to speak up for helpless individuals who are being unjustly treated. That would certainly include many minorities in America during the civil rights era. I am not implying that all of the injustice has vanished, but certainly things have improved enormously. There is still much work to be done and it is much more likely to be successful if it is based on progress rather than grievances.

As our nation has tried to move away from God, godly principles have fallen by the wayside. This has provided an opening for cruelty and indifference toward those in need, and indeed toward anyone who disagrees with the "woke" agenda. It will be up to the faith community to forcefully advocate for godly principles of tolerance and love once again. It is those principles that will allow harmony to once again flourish throughout our land. It is those principles that will keep us from being influenced by the purveyors of hatred who encourage us to cancel our peaceful neighbors who have a different political yard sign on their lawn. It is our love for our children, our grandchildren, and all of those who come after us that will give us the courage to fight for the freedoms that were given to us by our Creator, as was so eloquently described in the Declaration of Independence. And it was these principles that inspired the faith-based community to rise up in great numbers and to dedicate great resources in support of the civil rights movement. I dare say that without that kind of determination and fortitude, we would still be in the dark ages in regard to racial relationships in America.

Now we have a job once again for the faith-based community, and that is to help the American population recognize that we are not each other's enemies. We are an incredibly powerful nation with the ability to resist any external adversaries, but we have not noticed the creation of internal enemies who are probably more dangerous. Internal divisiveness requires the attention of all who wish for the survival of our nation. Sermons emanating from the pulpits of America and church-sponsored community activities must now vigorously promote caring about one's neighbor and promoting a healthy environment that is conducive to success. That means devoting talent and resources to neighborhoods in places like Chicago where shootings are through the roof and many of the young men are placed in untenable situations where they either have to join a gang or be harassed and perhaps even killed. The social groups that claim to care about Black lives are doing nothing and yet these precious souls are being used as nothing but pawns, and as Proverbs 24 states, they are being drawn unto death and are ready to be slain. This is a time for the church to once again become active in lifting so many individuals with great potential out of a desperate situation.

One of the reasons why the previous administration started HUD's "Mustard Seed" program was to take advantage of the fact that churches reside in the midst of communities with great social needs. They will be able to assist the needy and develop the kind of relationships with people that government agencies are simply incapable of. The government, however, can support them and can craft programs that will help the largest number of people become self-sufficient. That is the kind of civil rights program that really makes a difference.

There are many examples of how churches make a big difference, but one that particularly struck me was in Riverside, California. The church had some excess property and decided to build four single-family homes on that property for families experiencing homelessness. The church family provided everything that was needed by those families to help make them self-sufficient, usually within one year. It was a tremendously successful program and a great model for other churches. Families that are taken in by the church tend to feel a special obligation to be successful because they don't want to disappoint those who have invested so much in their well-being. That does not tend to be the case with government-supported programs.

By the same token, the support of the civil rights movement by the faith-based community created a very special bond that can quickly be reestablished to help rehabilitate violence-stricken, impoverished neighborhoods where hope has been lost.

I was recently talking to a family whose daughter was traumatized at her elementary school. She came home stating that she was ashamed of being white because of "white privilege." Young, impressionable white students are being made to feel like villains all over the country due to the teachings of a radical element intent on fundamentally changing our nation by indoctrinating our young people. This represents a prime opportunity for Christians to intervene with a message of hope and salvation. Even if some of our people have bought into the message of guilt and shame, through a relationship with Christ, those feelings can be erased, along with feelings of guilt and shame for virtually any other thing that has impacted one's life. The church also has an opportunity to resist the feelings of victimization afflicting the minority community as a result of the same indoctrination tactics that are used on white students. Christianity encourages excellence and self-reliance.

I well remember feelings of anguish and discouragement when I was a youngster because there was nothing but poverty and despair around me. When I began to put my trust in the Lord, it changed my entire perspective. I began to believe that I was going to be successful and that no human could stop me. Much of that change in attitude was secondary to relationships I developed with members of the faith-based community. That strong sense of morality, responsibility, self-reliance, and trusting God gave me the confidence to triumph over many obstacles that could easily have served as excuses for failure and reasons for victimization.

In the Old Testament of the Bible, the word "stranger" was frequently used when referring to someone of a different nation and ethnicity. The book of Leviticus makes it very clear that such individuals were not to be treated with racism but rather as members of one's own family. Leviticus 19:34 says, "But the stranger that dwelleth with you shall be unto you as one born among you, and thou shalt love him as thyself; for ye were strangers in the land of Egypt: I am the LORD your God." These types of Judeo-Christian directives leave little doubt about how we are to treat each other regardless of any differences that exist. Obviously, strangers are likely to have opinions that are different as well, and that should make no difference in how they are treated by someone with Christian love in their heart.

In the New Testament first book of John, chapter 4 says, "If a man say, I love God, and hateth his brother, he is a liar: for he that loveth not his brother whom he hath seen, how can he love God whom he has not seen? And this commandment have we from him, That he who loveth God love his brother also." I keep emphasizing this point to remove any doubt about biblical injunctions meant to eliminate any rationale for racism. The word of God specifically says you are a liar if you claim to have a relationship with Him and are a racist. It can't be much clearer than that.

Another interesting idea has recently surfaced in this country that is incompatible with biblical principles: the concept of universal basic income. This would mean that everybody over a certain age receives a basic income that would provide for the bare necessities of life. They would not have to do any work to receive this and it would be paid for by those who do work. What does the Bible say about such a plan? In 2 Thessalonians 3:10 the apostle Paul says, "For even when we were with you, this we commanded you, that if any would not work, neither should he eat." This biblical admonition clearly does not support the concept of welfare paid for by others in the case of people who are perfectly capable of working themselves. There are abundant instances of biblical admonitions to help those who cannot help themselves, but the biblical principle of self-reliance is incontrovertible. There is nothing cruel or unchristian about requiring people to become self-sufficient.

Some people have more difficulty than others at acquiring the necessary skills to support themselves, in which case a person motivated by the right spirit would invest some of their own time and effort in helping to prepare that individual to take care of themselves. Church communities are perfectly suited for these kinds of endeavors. Various other types of nonprofits and even some for-profit organizations can and should participate in preparing fellow citizens for the job market. When organizations combine forces, one might be able to provide childcare, while another can facilitate the obtaining of a GED where needed, and another may be able to train people with specific skills. When all of these organizations, including the church, are able to work with federal, state, and local government officials, the synergy provides a powerful tool to enhance the quality of life for citizens. This was one of my big takeaways after spending four years as the secretary of the U.S. Department of Housing and Urban Development.

From this discussion, we can see the amazing good that can be brought about by the religious community in our country. America is really quite different from any other nation in the world in the sense that we fully acknowledge the presence of God in our lives. Our founding document, the Declaration of Independence, speaks of certain unalienable rights provided to us by our Creator, a.k.a. God. Our Pledge of Allegiance says we are one nation under God. Every bill in our wallet and every coin in our pocket says, "In God We Trust." God is acknowledged in the stonework of many of our federal buildings and monuments. Churches decorate the landscape from coast to coast. Could this have something to do with the tremendous blessings this country has enjoyed for centuries now?

It was the presence of the United States of America

that turned the tide in the favor of freedom during World War II. It is the United States of America that has been on the forefront of resisting the forces of tyranny around the world. America acts as a stabilizing force to resist the worst tendencies of human nature. As Alexis de Tocqueville noted during his study of America in the 1830s, our churches played a great role in helping Americans establish a sense of morality and duty. But it is also important to realize that it is not just the religious structure established by various denominations that has helped us. It is a true belief in the power of God and the power of good. The power of God gives us the ability to do that which is good both individually and as a nation.

I vividly recall being in a very uncomfortable situation when I was a neurosurgery resident at Johns Hopkins many years ago. I was the resident on call when a young man was brought into the emergency room who had been severely beaten with a baseball bat. He was unconscious, and a CT scan revealed tremendous swelling of the brain along with hemorrhages in his brain. His only chance of survival was a risky operation in which portions of the frontal and temporal lobes of the brain would be removed. I had witnessed an operation like that before but had never performed one myself. There was a neurosurgical conference going on in another part of the country and most of the attending neurosurgeons were there. The attending who was left behind for some reason was not reachable by myself or the paging operator. I was left with a terrible dilemma. Should I try to perform a risky operation with no attending neurosurgeon, which was illegal but might save this young man's life, or should I play it safe with respect to my career aspirations? I asked God to give me the wisdom to know what to do and how to do it, and I took that young man to the operating room without an attending surgeon. I remembered with amazing clarity everything that needed to be done to alleviate the pressure in his skull and save his life. Today that young man is a psychologist and a counselor for young people. Instead of suffering consequences for my actions, I received praise and congratulations for doing the right thing. That's what God and religion can do and has done for us as a nation. And that is why Alexis de Tocqueville correlated America's greatness with America's goodness. The source of that goodness is in the heart of each of us.

CHAPTER 10

Is It Racism or Classism?

As a child growing up in Detroit in a single-parent home after my parents' divorce, my dream was to be middle class. Most of the kids in my school came from two-parent homes and enjoyed a lower-middle-class existence. They frequently had a dime or a nickel or sometimes even a quarter to spend on candy and other treats. Periodically the homeroom teacher would announce that popcorn balls would be available for purchase the next day at five cents each. They were about the size of a baseball and were wrapped in colorful cellophane. Some kids would purchase an entire bag of popcorn balls for a dollar. Throughout the entire elementary school experience, I was never able to purchase a popcorn ball because we had no extra money. They looked so delicious, but I tried to act like I didn't really want one. I desperately wanted one, but what I wanted more than that was to be like everyone else and not always be on the outside looking in. To my immature mind, all that was required was to achieve middle-class standing. But what is that in actuality?

There are those who say that America does not have a class system and that everyone is equal. If that were the case, how did the term "middle class" become a standard part of the American lexicon? How can you have a middle class without having an upper class and a lower class? Obviously, we do have a class system, as does virtually every society throughout history in every part of the world regardless of what they call it. For example, in many parts of Africa people arrived at a social gathering based on their class. The very lowest-class individuals arrived early. The middle-class people arrived on time. And those at the top of the hierarchical ladder arrived late, with their degree of lateness being carefully observed.

Traditionally in America class is determined by a combination of income, wealth, occupation, education, and social networks. Many people try to define it strictly on the basis of income, which is probably the biggest factor, but the other factors still significantly impact one's status in our society. For example, a well-known professor of philosophy at Princeton whose net worth is only $800,000 and whose annual income is only $150,000 would still be considered upper class by many, particularly if he was involved with the "right" social networking entities.

An illiterate sanitation worker who won the lottery and suddenly had $10 million might have a hard time being accepted as a member of the upper class.

The vast majority of Americans fit into the middle-class category. Although class structure in America is described in many different ways, for the purposes of this discussion I would describe it as follows:

- Upper class: people with the ability to buy whatever they want, travel wherever they want to go, and generally do as they please without the need for a regular paycheck.
- Middle class: people who have to work and save and plan in order to purchase their desires within reason, travel where they want to go within reason, and follow their dreams.
- Lower class: people with low skill levels, low educational attainment, and incomes that allow them to survive, but generally not enough to save or invest.

Obviously not everyone fits neatly into these three categories, but they will accommodate the vast majority of Americans. One of the things that has made America such an attractive destination for people around the world has been the ability of most people to achieve middle-class status here as long as they are willing to dedicate themselves to such a goal. In my case, growing up in poverty was a great motivator to work even harder whenever I faced obstacles that might have precluded my dream of obtaining middle-class status. I am fortunate and extremely grateful that my ascension did not end with middle-class status. Many others have also been able to move from class to class based on choices they made and the amount of energy they were willing to expend to achieve their goals. That, of course, is at the very core of capitalism.

Traditionally the personal efforts that led to great achievements have been something widely admired in America regardless of ethnicity. I say traditionally because more recently there have been many who are more concerned about the welfare of the group than about the welfare of the individual. They have demanded equality of outcome more than equality of opportunity. This is the basic difference between capitalism and communism. In the view of communists, the government should own and control all sources of income generation and distribution. Resources should be distributed on the basis of need, with only minor consideration given to talent. This system, which has been tried in various nations throughout the world, has never produced a nation like America with widespread contentment and accumulation of personal resources. There also has never been a nation as generous as America. We have a plethora of charitable organizations and individuals that are dedicated to providing for those who cannot provide for themselves.

Naturally the question arises, "Which system is better?" One that allows ownership based on effort and ability, where some people who lack the ability or the will to put forth effort can suffer, or a system where only the elite rulers own and control things, but the rest of the populace, although relatively poor, has their basic needs taken care of? In the latter system, which is supposedly classless, there are only two classes: the rulers and the ruled.

Beneath the bickering and headlines about racial injustice and accusations of inappropriate police behavior lies the argument about capitalism versus communism. There was a time in the not-too-distant past when Democrats and Republicans still fought like crazy because they had different approaches to reaching the same goal. Now they have very different goals, with one group pushing very hard for government solutions to everything from education to living environment to health care to leisure activities, and the other group focusing on the rights of individuals and the localities in which they reside. This is the reason that in today's very partisan atmosphere you see straight party-line votes on many issues that come before Congress. In a way this dichotomy is good because it gives the American people a chance to make a clear decision about which form of government they prefer.

Our founders were very cognizant of the fact that these kinds of situations would arise, and they structured our voting options in such a way that the people would be able to make the ultimate decision through our electoral system. They perhaps did not foresee the manipulation of the population by big tech and most of the media, which of course does not provide a true picture for the populace and therefore leads to erroneous vote casting. That, coupled with the fact that voting irregularities have been documented many times and there is great suspicion regarding the integrity of our national voting system, puts us in a precarious position. Usually if there is cheating going on, the cheaters will proclaim the purity of the current voting system, not wishing to see a change. Whether that is going on now or not, it is imperative for the continued functioning of our democratic republic that we do everything possible to ensure the integrity of our voting system and restore confidence therein. This is a matter of great urgency that should be clear to all. This is not a time for cowardice by any of the three branches of our government regarding this issue. Everyone must be willing to take an open and very transparent look at every aspect of our electoral system and make changes where needed.

What does all of this have to do with racism or classism? Actually, the intersection is quite significant. Upper-class and middle-class people generally are much more engaged in voting than those in the lower classes. This is true for a variety of reasons, but recently some members of the political class have learned how to get ballots into the hands of those who don't usually vote and incentivize them to cast votes, usually in a certain direction. We have seen a lot of this occurring recently in Black neighborhoods, particularly during very important votes. As long as it is done in a certain way, it can be done legally. It is much easier to manipulate the voter in the privacy of their home than it would be at a public voting booth. This is one of the issues that must be adjudicated during the transparent analysis of our voting system.

We want as many people as possible to vote, but we also want a vote that is not manipulated in any way. Preying upon the emotions of Black people by telling them that their vote is being suppressed because people are insisting on transparency is a dishonest political tactic. It is appalling, but since it is so common, the tactic is largely ignored. Doing anything that discourages or impedes the vote of any group of people is also abhorrent, and whenever such things occur, they should be loudly condemned by everyone. The real issue we are talking about here is honesty and decency. These are traits that should be held up by both political parties for the sake of our country.

This side of heaven, there is unlikely ever to be a classless society. People seem to have an inexorable drive to establish group hierarchies, which inform relationships within that society. I have frequently heard Americans ridiculing the British because of the reverence they hold for the royal family. We say the whole concept of royalty is ridiculous and everyone is equal. The same Americans practically faint when they see a prominent movie star or superstar athlete. The point is, we all engage in some type of recognition of class structure. By recognizing and acknowledging that, it might be possible to eliminate some of the charges of racism that might be strictly attributable to classism, not that one is any better than the other. I have clearly witnessed in my own life situations where I was ignored when it was thought that I was a nobody, but that completely changed when it was discovered that I was a Yalie or a brain surgeon or both.

I remember one time when I was in the market for a new Jaguar. I walked into a dealership and started looking at the cars on the showroom floor. There were three salesmen having a conversation elsewhere in the showroom and they completely ignored me for about forty minutes, after which time I left in disgust. I went to a different dealership where I was immediately recognized and served and subsequently paid cash for a new Jaguar. Usually if someone walks into a luxury car dealership in a suit and tie, the dealers would assume that they were a person of means and they would be stumbling over each other to see who could be the first person to get there. Since their living is based on commissions, it is reasonable to assume that their lack of enthusiasm for my presence was secondary to their assumption that I really couldn't afford a new Jaguar. There was no basis for them to draw that conclusion other than the color of my skin. That was an instance where their racism came at a cost personally to them. I suspect that if they had known that I was serious about buying a Jaguar and had the money to do so, they would not have given my skin color a second thought, but their cultural biases caused them to falsely predetermine my class status and act accordingly.

Many on the progressive left have claimed that it is

extremely difficult to climb the rungs of the class ladder. They claim that almost everyone in America belonging to one of the lower classes will remain there for the rest of their lives. They claim that the American dream is a myth designed to give people false hope and manipulate them into cooperation. I suspect that there may be some projection there. Rags-to-riches stories abound in America precisely because here it is much easier than in most places to move up the class ladder. As I mentioned in an earlier chapter, as a child I hated poverty. Once I discovered that through my own efforts I could move well beyond economic poverty, poverty no longer bothered me. Was I being naïve as the left-wing progressives would have you believe, or was I preparing like millions of others to realize the American dream?

The first big change in economic lifestyle for me occurred when I stepped onto the campus of Yale University. Even though I was still from an impoverished background, I was able to live just like the kids belonging to the wealthiest families in the world. Because I was a Yale student, I was treated with deference wherever I went. That continued to be the case throughout medical school and my residency training at Johns Hopkins. Even though interns and residents make meager salaries, my wife, Candy, worked as a trust officer for a bank and as an editorial assistant for a scientific journal, which allowed us to lead a middle-class lifestyle. When I became an attending neurosurgeon at Johns Hopkins in 1984 after having spent a year in Australia as the senior registrar at the major teaching hospital in Western Australia, we were thrust into the upper middle class with respect to income. Over the course of the next twenty-nine years not only did I enjoy major salary increases, but I joined two Fortune 500 corporate boards, became a highly compensated public speaker, and wrote a number of books, a few of which were number one *New York Times* bestsellers. That, along with real estate investments and other ventures, easily lifted us into the upper class. Now I could afford all the popcorn balls I wanted. Interestingly, however, I discovered that once you can afford pretty much anything you want, the desire for many of those material things dissipates. This is particularly the case for those like myself who enjoy a strong relationship with the Lord and derive joy from doing His will.

Throughout all those years of social class ladder climbing, I never felt as if someone was discriminating against me. That is not to say that I did not have some difficulties with some people. I also faced some difficult circumstances from time to time, but I did not ascribe these to racism like some people have a tendency to do. People tend to find what they expect to see. If you think someone hates you, in most cases you will interpret whatever they say or do in light of your expectation. It may have absolutely nothing to do with them hating you, but you will perceive it as such. Those who see racism in everything will continue to condemn everything as racist. I can hear the critics now saying, "Carson is looking at the world through rose-colored glasses and sees no prejudice because he doesn't want to see it." I do not believe that to be the case, but if it is, wouldn't my existence be much more pleasant than that of someone who interpreted all the same things in a negative light?

My childhood desire to reach middle-class status was obviously reached and surpassed. But those aspirations have also been realized by millions of other Americans, both white and minority. According to the Brookings Institution, in 1979, 84 percent of the middle class was white, with 9 percent being Black, 5 percent Latino, and 2 percent other. By 2019 the middle class as defined by the Brookings Institution was 59 percent white, 12 percent Black, 18 percent Latino, and 10 percent other. The social demographics of our nation are changing rapidly and most likely will continue to do so. Certainly, as people mix and mingle, stereotypes will begin to fade, and as has been in the past, people will tend to associate with the people they know. This is one of the reasons why things like interracial marriage have become much more prevalent in our society. Nevertheless, those silly stereotypes still exist, and it would be beneficial if people could adopt a more tolerant attitude toward others who make serious blunders secondary to believing in those stereotypes.

For example, I have a friend who was a highly decorated Black military general. While he was checking into a hotel, one of the other customers, who was white, motioned for him to fetch his luggage. My friend had on a military uniform and because he was Black was mistaken for a bellhop. He did not get angry, but simply introduced himself and tried to alleviate the horrible embarrassment that white gentleman felt. It very much reminds me of the numerous times that I was mistaken for an orderly because I had on scrubs and a white coat. By being kind instead of getting horribly offended, I believe it is possible to make a bigger impression on the person who made the mistake and increase the likelihood that such a thing will never happen again. There are plenty of instances where people make mistakes about a person's social status not because they are racists, but rather because they are acting or speaking based on all of their prior experiences. The person who is the object of their mistake can react angrily and even violently, or they can choose to assume an educational role to move the violator to a better place. It is actually more fun to watch the violator try to recover than it is to make them suffer a tongue-lashing that does nothing for anyone.

Over the course of the years, I have had an opportunity to get acquainted with a large number of very wealthy individuals from many ethnic backgrounds. Most of the ones we know are very nice people who are just like anybody else and wish to be treated like normal people. The majority of them, however, tend to associate mostly with other people in their socioeconomic class. This is not necessarily because they are snobs or racists, but in many cases they have found themselves subject to requests for financial assistance when they deal with people who are not wealthy. That is something that is hard for people who do not fit into the upper class to understand. Most of our wealthy friends engage in a significant amount of charitable giving and many of the well-known charities in our country could not exist without this kind of support. When surveys are done, America is usually number one or certainly among the top few countries when it comes to charitable giving. It's part of our DNA and is one of the reasons that we shouldn't envy or wish ill on our wealthy fellow citizens who contribute greatly in their own way to the welfare of our nation.

Are wealthy people treated differently and better than most other people? Of course they are. They are much more likely to provide a substantial donation or a big tip or some other manifestation of wealth. It is not hard to understand why hotels and other business establishments have special concierge arrangements for their wealthy clients. Many hospitals have a special concierge program that entails numerous perks for the wealthy. In turn, many hospitals, universities, training academies, and public facilities bear the names of very wealthy contributors. Who builds factories, manufacturing facilities, entertainment complexes, training facilities, and on and on? Obviously, the answer is the wealthy. In many cases they do it because they want to increase their wealth, but in the process they provide multitudinous jobs and opportunities for others. We should celebrate the success of the wealthy rather than attempt to confiscate their wealth for the good of everyone else as is dictated by Marxist philosophy.

On the surface what the communists advocate sounds good to some. They say that no one should need basic things like food, shelter, and health care, among other things. They feel those things should be provided to everyone regardless of their level of contribution to societal needs. On the other hand, in 2 Thessalonians 3:10 the Bible says if you don't work, you don't eat. Obviously, the Bible needs to be read contextually rather than just pulling out random verses. The Bible speaks in many places about compassion for those who are in need, but it also emphasizes work and dedication to excellence. It does not mince words when it comes to those who are slothful and lazy. In the United States we have a combination of work ethic and socialistic programs to provide a safety net rather than a guarantee for those in need. It is a system that has worked relatively well and provided a standard of living that remains the envy of the world.

Can such a system withstand the withering criticism of those who want to fundamentally change it and who have overwhelming access to the means of communicating their ideas? Jealousy and envy unfortunately are traits that are widely disseminated throughout humanity. When the airwaves are full of people calling for the rich to pay their fair share when they already pay the lion's share of all taxes, those tendencies toward envy are only enhanced and dissatisfaction with the system grows exponentially. If those wishing to change our society can create the perception of massive dysfunction that is caused by inequitable distribution of goods and services, they can gain the support of the people for the creation of massive government programs that provide for the needs of every citizen at the expense of the "evil rich." This certainly is not a new tactic and has been used in many places throughout the world to effect a change in governing structures.

We are currently facing a serious challenge to the continuation of our system of governance as a democratic republic. Perhaps that is what Benjamin Franklin realized as he was exiting the building in 1787 at the conclusion of the Constitutional Convention and was asked, "What have we got here, a Republic or a monarchy?" He reportedly answered, "A Republic, if you can keep it." This response is often quoted by both Democrats and Republicans as they try to justify their policy pursuits. Benjamin Franklin was an extraordinarily wise individual who thought deeply about issues and was a great proponent of the system we put in place. He was also a great student of history and knew that such a system would undergo severe challenges and could only persist if the American people had the courage to utilize their newly penned Constitution to protect their rights. Hopefully as one nation under God, our republic will survive.

In the early days of our nation, it was erroneously concluded that only well-heeled citizens who were landowners had the intellectual wherewithal to understand

and vote on issues of societal governance. With those kinds of requirements in place, the bodies making decisions for everyone generally consisted only of white males. They were at the pinnacle of the class structure, which was vigorously enforced. Those who deny a class structure in America need only go back and study the system that existed from the very beginnings of our nation. However, the existence of a distorted and unfair system in the past does not condemn our current system and require its dismantling, as some propose. Wise people learn from their mistakes and the mistakes of others. We have an opportunity in our country to really emphasize the things existent in our founding documents—namely, the principle that "all men are created equal." This means we should strive for a society that treats everyone with dignity and fairness regardless of their occupation, educational attainment, or bank balance. Such a pursuit would certainly be consistent with our Judeo-Christian values and would facilitate the unification of our country.

When we successfully abolish class distinctions, a lot of what is perceived as racism will also disappear. A good friend of mine who has passed on was a prominent neurosurgeon in California who happened to be Black. He loved gardening and had a beautiful rose garden in his front yard that could be seen from the street. One day as he was pruning his garden a passerby asked him how much he was paid for the lovely job he did. They were thinking that perhaps they might be able to hire him to do work at their estate. He chuckled and replied, "I get to sleep with the lady of the house." Fortunately, he did not leave them struggling with that comment but went on to explain that he was the owner of that beautiful estate and enjoyed doing his own gardening. Was the person making the inquiry a racist? I'm not sure you can make that determination on the basis of that single encounter. But we can determine that the person made an inappropriate assumption that was probably based on race.

Many of us have preconceived notions of who people are based on their appearance and the activities in which they are engaged. We also frequently make assessments of people based on their skin color and the environment. That was the case with the Black general who was mentioned earlier in this chapter. As an attending physician and chief of pediatric neurosurgery at Johns Hopkins, I can remember occasions when I would evaluate patients and engage in conversations with their parents, who at some point would ask me, "When is Dr. Carson coming?" Even though I would have introduced myself in the beginning, they were expecting an older white doctor and had paid little attention to that introduction. Was this racism or innocent capitulation to one's expectations? I suspect the latter, and in virtually all cases, after some initial embarrassment a warm and comfortable relationship was established. Interestingly, there were some cases early in my career where Black parents were uncomfortable with the idea of me operating on their child. I believe they had been brainwashed to believe that white doctors were more competent since they had not achieved their position on the basis of affirmative action. As I became better known and celebrated, of course, those kinds of interactions ceased completely, but it does remind us that false narratives about competence and race still leave their ugly scars on our society.

As we have discussed, a class system clearly does exist in America. It has endured since the beginning of our nation and is inconsistent with our founding documents that declare the equality of all mankind. Because designating one group of people as more important than another group can and generally does lead to societal conflict, we would be wise to seriously embrace the concept of equality. Treating everyone as an equal not only feels better, but would deal a death blow to racism. We should therefore make a very conscious effort to eliminate preferential treatment based on wealth. This is not to say that wealthy people should not be able to purchase whatever they can afford, but it is to say that God loves everyone equally and has paid the price through His Son to save everyone. When compared to the wealth and power of God, a pauper and the wealthiest man on earth are roughly the same.

I cannot emphasize enough the fact that there is nothing wrong with wealth and with high achievement. In fact, we should celebrate those things, particularly in a society that makes them available to anyone. We must continue to maintain a system that allows people to determine their own aspirations as well as how much effort they wish to dedicate to the accomplishment of those dreams. If, as Benjamin Franklin implied, we are to maintain our republic, we cannot give credence to those who are sowing seeds of division and driving wedges between every demographic group in our nation in their attempt to foster hatred for our system of governance while placing their utopian dream of complete government care and control on a false pedestal of peace and tranquility.

We cannot dwell on the mistakes that were committed by imperfect people in our past. We will continue to make mistakes, because we are human, but let us not forget what every coin in our pocket and every bill in our wallet says: "In God We Trust." We must never forget the godly principles that were foundational to the establishment of our country. Those include:

- Love thy neighbor as thyself. This means we treat those around us the same way we would like to be treated ourselves. It clearly does not mean trying to hurt those around us if they don't agree with us. The whole concept of cancel culture is inspired by evil and has no place in a nation like ours. We need to remember that if two people agree about everything, one of them is unnecessary. You will always learn more from people who can disagree with you than from bootlickers and yes-men.
- Care for those who cannot care for themselves. There will always be people who for physical or mental reasons are incapable of caring for themselves. Our

Judeo-Christian values make it imperative for us to provide the necessities of life for such individuals. Proactively caring for such people generally is less costly to the society than ignoring them. On the other hand, taking care of the needs of people who can easily do so on their own is not only unnecessary but destructive, because it creates dependency and diminishes human potential.
- Develop our God-given potential in order to be useful to those around us. We are created in the image of God and have enormously sophisticated brains capable of unimaginable things if those brains are properly programmed.
- Have values and principles that govern our lives. Even natives in the deepest, darkest jungles have a sense of right and wrong. That is why they frequently wait until nighttime to commit robbery. If our civilization is to advance, we must have standards of behavior that acknowledge the difference between right and wrong.

Having a class system and being a classy person are two completely different things. You can be a billionaire and be completely classless or you can be a pauper who is the epitome of class. Best of all, you can be an ordinary American or citizen of the world who cares about your fellow man.

CHAPTER 11

Education, the Great Equalizer

THE FOUNDERS OF THIS COUNTRY FELT that it was most suitable for an educated and informed populace. There was a great deal of emphasis on literacy and education in general. I have found that perhaps the greatest gift you can provide to someone who wants to succeed in our society is a good education. Even some of the most historically evil components of our society recognized the importance of education, since slave owners and their political lackeys made it illegal to teach slaves how to read or to otherwise educate them. They clearly understood that you would not be able to continue to dominate people who were educated and who understood their rights as human beings.

In our country there were many who fought vigorously for educational rights for all of our citizens, including

Blacks. During the period immediately following the emancipation of the slaves, numerous educational facilities were created for the purpose of giving the newly freed American citizens a chance for success in the free enterprise system that existed. Blacks were eager to take advantage of these opportunities and many quickly rose to prominence, with some entering the political arena during Reconstruction. The rapid progress of Blacks was so stunning that many southern whites felt threatened and began to put in place measures to restrict their social progress. They were particularly concerned about the possibility of large numbers of Black citizens being able to vote and determine the power structures of local governments, hence the formation of the Jim Crow laws that complicated election procedures with insurmountable barriers for potential Black voters.

A number of Black institutions of higher learning were established, some of which have thrived and remain active today. The previous presidential administration put a lot of emphasis on historically Black colleges and universities (known as HBCUs) and provided long-term funding for them. The previous president of the United States felt that the heads of these HBCUs had better things to do with their time than annually devoting huge amounts of resources and effort to securing funding from the federal government. These institutions try to maintain an atmosphere that fosters pride in African American history and traditions. They do not exclude whites or people of other ethnicities and play a very important role in educating many citizens of our nation.

My mother was from a very large rural family in Tennessee and never finished the third grade. She was essentially illiterate, but she very cleverly hid that from most people, including my brother and me for many years. She did, however, value education highly and was very distraught when my brother, Curtis, and I brought home bad grades and evidence of academic failure. She struggled to teach herself how to read and actually got her GED and matriculated at a college well after I had obtained my bachelor's degree from Yale and moved on to medical school at the University of Michigan. In 1994 she was awarded an honorary doctorate degree and was proudly able to proclaim, "I'm Dr. Carson too." She was perhaps the wisest person I have ever known, and fully recognized that my life and the life of my brother would be severely hampered if we did not avail ourselves of the best education we could possibly get. Unfortunately, as a youngster, I did not share her zeal for academic pursuits. It was not until she forced me to read book after book and submit to her written book reports, which she could not even read, that I realized how important arming oneself with knowledge could be in the pursuit of success.

Curtis and I were latchkey kids without a great deal of adult supervision after school. Our mother was going from job to job cleaning other people's houses and babysitting. She frequently left the house at five in the morning and did not return until midnight. Curtis and I became walking television guides. We knew what was coming on every channel virtually every hour of the day. If we had devoted the same amount of time and energy to our schoolwork, I'm sure we would have been stellar students. When my mother saw our first report cards after we returned from Boston, she was horrified. She knew how hard she had to work and how few opportunities she had because of her lack of education, and now she saw that scenario possibly being repeated in our lives. She desperately prayed for wisdom because she had no idea what to do. After that she began to notice that the houses that she cleaned contained large numbers of books and that the owners spent a lot of time reading. Although she couldn't read the books, she was duly impressed that they contained the secrets of success. Despite much criticism from her friends, she imposed strict limitations on television watching and required Curtis and me to read two books from the Detroit public libraries every week and submit written book reports to her. To say we were disgruntled would be a major understatement, but we had no choice in the matter. Many people have noted that Black boys growing up in the inner city with no father figure are handicapped by the fact that they have no authority figures in their lives. They clearly did not know my mother.

Although I did not want to read the books, I was always looking at words, and suddenly my spelling abilities improved dramatically. Since I needed to put those words together, my grammatical skills also improved significantly. However, the most important benefit from reading was the perspective that I gained by delving into the lives of numerous successful people. After reading many books about nature, which I loved, I started reading about people, including inspirational figures like Booker T. Washington, who was no fan of victimhood. As I read about various scientists and entrepreneurs and doctors, I began to understand that the kind of success they experienced was not automatic and required in-depth study and hard work. Both Curtis and I became very studious, and instead of turning on the television when we got home from school, we couldn't wait to get to our library books. I was always reading and acquired the nickname "Bookworm."

Even though we were surrounded by people who proclaimed vigorously that society was unfair and that my academic pursuits would end in disappointment, I refused to be deterred and was convinced that I would in fact become a doctor. I envisioned myself having a nice office, driving nice cars, living in a beautiful ranch-style home, and being an important part of the local community. Essentially, I began living in a world apart from the one that defined my day-to-day existence.

In addition to book learning, I started spending a lot of time in museums and at local universities acquiring a great deal of cultural knowledge that was foreign to most of my classmates. Even though they teased me a lot and called me Poindexter, I believe that most of them had deep admiration for my determination, and in the mock elections held during my senior year in high school, I was voted not only "most studious" but also "most likely to succeed." That indicates that even though I was the subject of ridicule, many of my classmates, deep in their souls, knew that there was a great benefit associated with the serious pursuit of academic excellence.

Something that needs attention sooner rather than later is the negative peer pressure found in many disadvantaged minority school systems where the academically gifted students often find themselves hiding their accomplishments from fellow students to avoid criticism and accusations of "acting white." This is akin to the crabs-in-a-barrel phenomenon where the crabs in the bottom of the barrel grab and pull down any crab that is trying to crawl out. Those students applying the peer pressure have no idea that they are tools being used to perpetuate victimhood and dependency. These are the same students who readily buy into the notion put forth by proponents of CRT and similar theories that being on time or caring about accuracy in mathematical calculations is a trait of the dominant and oppressive white society and should be rejected. Subsequently, when students who buy into this foolishness are rejected in the job market for tardiness or inaccuracy, claims of racism abound.

Many people, Black, white, and other, sacrificed their freedom, their health, and even in some cases their lives in the fight for equal education for Black people in America. They would turn over in their graves if they knew how difficult it was to get many of the very people they fought for to actually take advantage of the rights that were secured with their blood. Instead of listening to the voices of victimhood and revenge, we should hear the souls of those who understood that true freedom will only be maintained by those who avail themselves of the knowledge of how the ecosystem in which they exist operates, and that understanding comes through education.

If you stop and think about it, it is totally unreasonable to fail to prepare oneself for a well-paying job and then complain about not being hired. If one has not acquired the necessary education and training to be successful in that position, their concentration should be on rectifying that situation quickly and then reapplying. Nevertheless, we still hear lots of complaints of unfairness in hiring. As a society we should fully support complaints of unfairness if someone is precluding a certain segment of the population from having the opportunity to get the education and training they need to be successful. There is a big difference between denying someone the opportunity for appropriate training and denying someone who is not educated and trained and yet still feels they should be hired.

I am reminded of a society reentry program in Jacksonville, Florida, where prison inmates were given education, training, and a job to which they could report as soon as they were released. Those trainees did such a stellar job that multiple other employers entered the program, with similar highly satisfactory results. These are the kinds of things that we as a society need to be thinking about. So many of the young people who end up in the penal system did not have good role models or adequate parental guidance as they matured. This left them vulnerable to the influences of the street, and although many of them have great potential, those negative influences landed them in jail. If attention is not directed to rehabilitating them, that first prison encounter is often the beginning of a hardening process that is very difficult to reverse. Yet the beaming faces that I have witnessed on those inmates who were fortunate enough to be placed in caring rehabilitation programs tell me that we as a society should make it our goal to rehabilitate every single one of these young people, since they can be an important part of the workforce and in some cases will make outstanding contributions to society.

Also, when you give someone hope, you also give them energy to pursue their dreams. A hopeless person is a pitiful sight, and that is one of the reasons we should fight so hard against those forces in our society that are trying to convince people that they are hopeless victims of an evil and racist nation. I vividly remember my hopelessness and hatred of poverty rapidly fading away as I read the biographies of highly successful people. Knowing that I could emulate their success through my own efforts without dependency on anyone else helped me to realize that living in poverty was a temporary situation, because I had the power to change it.

Much of my own education was self-education. It was not uncommon for my teachers in high school to be distracted from the intended presentation because they were too busy enforcing discipline. I had to travel around the city of Detroit to many different venues to gain the kind of education that I desired. I vividly remember being involved in forensic speech competitions, which were very helpful in teaching me to be comfortable in front of an audience. Those lessons, however, required me to travel many miles away from my home and my high school several times each month. Even though it was inconvenient, you have to consider that it's not going to be inconvenient for an extended period of time, but the benefit you derive from it will be lifelong.

Learning about jazz and Motown was easy in my environment, but learning about Baroque art and Mozart required a significant amount of extra effort. How does that extra effort impact one's life? Knowledge is power, and the more of it you have, the more power you have and the more connections and relationships you are able to develop. My wife, Candy, and I would have never gotten together if we hadn't both had an interest in classical music. We were both from Detroit but had to go to New Haven, Connecticut, for our common interests to intersect and bring us together. Over the course of many years, Candy and I have developed many friendships with very powerful and influential people because of our broad cultural interests.

America is a multicultural nation that has its own distinct culture. It is the merging of so many different heritages that has given us unparalleled strength when we are willing to work together. Some people are very homogeneous when it comes to relationships with others, and of course they have that choice, but they are missing out on a lot of wonderful experiences when they are unwilling to increase their social outreach into other cultures. Just the delightful culinary experiences themselves are worth any potential discomfort in reaching out to fellow Americans with different cultural heritages.

When it comes to self-education and education in general, it is very likely that you will learn many things you didn't know before from people of different cultures. The tremendous added benefit to cultural outreach is the obliteration of stereotypes and falsehoods that frequently lead to undesirable biases that are completely unjustified. As an exercise, if you really want to have some fun, try purposefully reaching out to someone or a family of a different culture. Invite them to your home for a home-cooked meal or schedule an outing that gives both families an opportunity to mingle with each other. I can virtually guarantee you that there will be learning on both sides and a good time will be had by all.

The formative years when small children are absorbing information like dry sponges are a time for maximal parental involvement. There are some on the progressive side who feel that this is the time when educators should be determining what the children are taught. In communist countries, the indoctrination of young children is foundational to the continuation of their power. Throughout grade school, elementary school, and high school the brain is still developing and it is so important that it be programmed correctly, because children are in the process of determining who they are and what they believe during those formative years.

When I was still practicing medicine, I would encounter many parents who asked my advice about taking recommended medications, because their child had been diagnosed with attention deficit hyperactivity disorder (ADHD). When I was a child in school, it was a relatively rare diagnosis, and now, of course, it is probably overdiagnosed. I generally told parents to try an experiment for three months before putting them on medications. The experiment would involve weaning them off so much television and video games while gradually increasing the amount of time they spent reading and discussing what they were reading with their parents. I didn't do any formal studies, but I was very impressed with the number of parents who came back three months later and reported that their child no longer seemed to be suffering from any disorder involving attention.

It is not hard to understand why so many children are misdiagnosed with ADHD. Frequently children are put in front of the television as soon as they are able to sit up. They watch a screen on which things are rapidly changing all the time. Then when they're old enough to handle the controls, they are given video games to entertain themselves. Again, everything is changing every few seconds to maintain their attention. Then when they are five or six years old, they are sent off to kindergarten, where the teacher is not changing into something every few seconds, yet they are expected to be attentive. It's not hard to imagine why they might not pay attention for very long.

Many parents have great difficulty separating their children from video games, which are very exciting. Can you imagine what is going to happen when virtual reality becomes commonplace and people can literally lose themselves in a virtual world of their choosing? As a society, we need to start thinking now about how to prevent people from getting lost in a fantasy world and neglecting the real one. On the other hand, when students can put on a headset and visit the ancient Roman Coliseum or witness a battle during the French and Indian War, it will make an indelible impression, and it is possible that learning may occur at a much more rapid pace.

Learning to use technology appropriately will be a major challenge for mankind in the future as well as now. We have already seen that there is not nearly as much emphasis on memorization in today's world because everybody carries on their hip in the form of an iPhone or some other smartphone a complete encyclopedia. There is no such thing as a senior moment anymore because Siri can give you the answer as soon as you ask the question. But this kind of instant access to information can be problematic if the source of the information is biased. We must be vigilant and vigorously push back against the dissemination of information meant for the purposes of indoctrination, especially when this occurs in a formal educational setting.

In the early days of 2021, I, along with some spectacular members of my HUD staff, formed a think tank / do tank called the American Cornerstone Institute. Its purpose is to emphasize the four major cornerstones that allowed our nation to go from a bunch of ragtag militiamen to the pinnacle of the world in record time. Those cornerstones are faith, liberty, community, and life. As we have moved away from them, turmoil and decay have made their presence felt. I hope you will visit americancornerstone.org and get involved in helping to preserve our wonderful nation. You will also notice a link to our "Little Patriots" program that teaches our young people the true history of our nation, warts and all. It is a free K–5 interactive learning program that can be accessed at littlepatriotslearning.com. The program is being expanded to include middle school and high school students, and the American Cornerstone Institute website also describes our "more perfect union" program for adult learning about the foundations of our nation.

Candy and I have three sons, all of whom are married with children. The oldest son, Murray, was born in Australia and trained as an engineer and also has a master's degree in information technology. The youngest son, Rhoeyce, is a CPA, and the middle son, Benjamin Junior, is an entrepreneur who owns or operates multiple businesses along with his wife, who is a physician. They are all very smart and accomplished young men.

When they were growing up, Benjamin Junior, or BJ as we call him, was always asking questions. After the question was answered, like clockwork his next question was "Why?" And the "whys" continued incessantly. It is actually very good to teach our young people to question what they are learning. They should know the basis for their beliefs rather than simply swallowing hook, line, and sinker everything they are told. In the Bible, we find wise counsel regarding this matter. Proverbs 14:15 says, "The simple believeth every word: but the prudent man looketh well to his going."

A good example of a question a young person who is facing indoctrination with CRT might ask is "If the vast majority of white people in America and particularly in the South did not own slaves, why do you demonize all white people as oppressors?" I suspect that the progressives who are pushing CRT would say that the white people who were slave owners were the ones who determined all the policies and created the foundations for our country, which of course is blatantly false and without factual authority. Authoritarian regimes do not like to be questioned and frequently impose penalties for even saying certain words or phrases. The purveyors of truth, on the other hand, have no problem being questioned, because they have nothing to hide.

As I mentioned earlier, my mother is probably the wisest person I have ever met even though she had very little in the way of formal learning. There is a big difference between wisdom and knowledge. There are many knowledgeable professors who do and say very foolish things. We recently witnessed one of the most foolish things ever done in the history of warfare when the president of the United States and his team evacuated our military forces from Afghanistan before extracting the people that they were protecting. That would be an unwise move regardless of which political party carried it out. One of the real characteristics of wise people is the ability to learn from other people's mistakes without making them all over again. This is perhaps the best reason to study our history rather than trying to erase the bad parts. All people and all societies make mistakes, but the wise ones learn from those mistakes, reducing the likelihood of a repetition.

I believe that one of the things that attracted so many people to the shores of America was the fact that we believed in people as individuals. Everyone had specific rights that they could freely exercise as long as they weren't infringing upon someone else's rights. That individuality also means that we learn differently. Some people get a great deal from listening to speeches and lectures, while others learn from reading, and still others may benefit the most from active discussions. I discovered that I am very visual and learn best by repetition. In medical school I had literally thousands of index cards with various sketches on them that I could review whenever I had a few minutes to kill. During my second year of medical school, I was living with my brother, Curtis, who was an engineering student, and even he knew all the bacteria and what they were sensitive to because I was always pulling out those cards. The earlier a student learns how they learn, the better they will do.

The individuality concept speaks volumes against generalization and groupthink. If everybody is an individual whose thoughts and ideas are cultivated by their environment and their past experiences, it makes no sense to group people together based on external physical features. The degree of ignorance that is required to judge people thusly is astronomical. Yet although vastly diminished, racism is alive and well and its last vestiges need to be stomped out.

Twenty-five years ago, Candy and I were so concerned about the state of education in America that we started our own scholarship fund. Initially it was called the USA Scholars Fund, but there were so many other "USA" funds that we yielded to the desires of the scholars themselves, who wanted to be called Carson scholars. The year 2021 is the twenty-fifth year in which we have given out scholarships to young people, starting in the fourth grade through high school, who achieve at the highest academic levels but who also demonstrate humanitarian qualities. It does society little good to have people who are very smart if they don't care about others. In 2021 we gave out the ten thousandth scholarship and in 2022 opened the 250th Ben

Carson reading room. These rooms are mostly in Title 1 schools and are designed to create a love for reading early in a child's educational journey. We also honor adults who are inspirational each year. In 2021 it was Lou Holtz, the legendary football coach, who is just brimming over with wisdom. Many very famous people have been the inspirational adult, and a complete listing of them, as well as other interesting material, can be found at carsonscholars.org.

Teaching our young people not only to be knowledgeable and wise, but also to be nice, is critical if our country is to avoid destruction. As I've noted before, Jesus Himself said, "A house divided against itself cannot stand." Some of the things going on in our country today are not only a far cry from the faith-based underpinnings of our founding, but are motivated by pure, unadulterated evil. When we have a government that is complicit with private organizations that target American citizens for cancellation if they don't toe the line, we have a real threat to our democratic republic. Deliberately trying to hurt people and their families over political disagreements is disgusting, but not unexpected, because we allowed the infiltration of political correctness and "woke"-ism into our society.

Now we will have to redouble our efforts to awaken the spirit of "love thy neighbor as thyself" that was such an integral part of our faith-based beginnings. I like to challenge audiences to find someone whom they normally don't talk to or associate with and try to do something nice for them. It can be challenging in the beginning, but it gets easier with time and it actually feels extremely good. If we can rekindle that spirit of community in our country, there is no power on earth that will be able to destroy us. Only we can destroy ourselves if we listen to the purveyors of hatred and division.

One trend that is growing extremely rapidly in our country is homeschooling. It was tremendously accelerated when parents all over the country began to realize that many of the public and even some of the private schools were teaching critical race theory as fact. Many of the teachers tried to hide the content of the doctrines they were teaching, but it eventually leaked out. Because many parents have significant teaching skills and real-world experience, they are able to take turns with teaching duties, which allows many of them to still hold down full-time jobs. Instead of teaching critical race theory, they can teach critical math theory and critical English theory and critical history theory and critical civics theory and critical science theory. The point is that school should be about preparing our young people for productive roles in society and not about turning them into radical iconoclasts.

Some have worried that homeschooling might not adequately prepare students for college. Having sat on a variety of admissions committees, I can tell you for sure that homeschoolers are generally better prepared, not less prepared, for higher education. The real question is, should they attend college, and if the answer to that is yes, what college should they attend? Many students go off to college as reasonable individuals and come back as radical extremists. It is well worth the time to do an in-depth study of the colleges and universities being considered for our precious young people. It is not too difficult to find out if people who think for themselves are mistreated on a particular campus. There is also a lot of information online about various professors and administrators of colleges and universities. An increasing number of colleges and universities, like Liberty University in Lynchburg, Virginia, have extensive online course offerings. Perhaps the best thing a parent can do before sending their young person off to college is to make sure they have a strong sense of self and a solid moral compass. The time to start ensuring those things is when they are toddlers, not when they are seniors in high school.

Most of our education as American citizens will occur outside of formal school settings. We learn every day when we converse with others and when we use social media. Many of us also gain a lot of information from television. There was a time when news anchors and correspondents tried to be objective. That time is largely gone now and it is important for the consumer to recognize the biases of reporters and networks. The problem with biased news is that it frequently leaves out important details that an informed individual should know. This occurs at a particularly high frequency around the time of important elections. If our freedoms are to be preserved in these perilous times, it will be necessary for American citizens and voters to arm themselves with knowledge. They must also know who they are voting for, rather than just looking for a familiar name on the ballot, which is what most people do. That leads to the repeated election of some people who are pretty far off in their thinking, yet they hold enormous power because they are always assured of reelection.

The whole point of education is to eradicate ignorance. Horrible things like racism are the result of ignorance. The better-educated and more well-rounded the society is, the less racism and other undesirable traits will be manifested. I have said some unflattering things about the media in this book, but I will say that recently, through commercials and various types of programming, the media has once again made attempts to stem the tide of racism. If they can be objective and not ideological, they are in a position to do a tremendous amount of good when it comes to race relationships. All of us have spheres of influence and can work within those spheres to create an atmosphere of love and tolerance, even for those with whom we disagree. We must remember that as a nation we have to compete with places like China that have four times as many people as we have. We cannot afford to be fighting each other and undereducating any segment of our population if we are to maintain our position in the world. I hope we will all manifest courage in our respective spheres of influence.

CHAPTER 12

The Path Forward

IS IT POSSIBLE FOR A MULTICULTURAL society to exist in a harmonious atmosphere, or are human beings just naturally selfish and domineering? I have had an opportunity to travel extensively throughout the world and have personally witnessed the peaceful coexistence of different racial groups in a shared social setting. I was in Singapore some years ago to participate in a complex surgical procedure and had an opportunity to work with medical staff from different ethnic groups, the predominant groups in that nation being Chinese, Indian, Malaysian, and other. Historically these groups have not always peacefully coexisted in Singapore. In fact, in the 1960s there were some violent race-related riots that claimed dozens of lives and injured many. That was before Singapore achieved nationhood.

The government recognized that the different ethnic groups were segregated into their own neighborhoods and there was very little cross-pollination. The government enacted many programs and policies to deliberately bring people together at the workplace, in educational facilities, and through recreation and other activities. It also made a concerted effort to establish and maintain freedom of religion since there were several dominant religious groups that previously had been in conflict with each other.

Singapore is a very heavily regulated society, but despite that, they have still been able to achieve a great deal of racial and religious harmony by encouraging integration and social interaction. I believe the same kind of harmony can be achieved anywhere without heavy government intervention if the emphasis is placed not on differences but rather on the things that the groups have in common. We, as Americans, have far more things that unite us than divide us. Unfortunately, the voices of division tend to have the microphones and portray themselves as righteous when in fact they are the ones who are sowing the seeds of discord. As long as we have power-hungry politicians and sycophantic media to advocate for them, we will have a very heavy lift to achieve harmony. But with much effort, I believe it is possible.

In my lifetime we have made enormous progress in racial relations in America. Today our society is completely different than it was when I was a child and witnessed "whites only" drinking fountains and lavatories in the

South. It is completely different from the time when one of my teachers chastised all the white students for allowing a Black student to be the number one academic achiever. It is completely different from the time when seeing a Black pilot flying a commercial airliner was a big deal. It is completely different than when a Black quarterback in the NFL was an oddity. I could obviously go on with this list for a long time, because major changes have occurred despite the fact that many on the progressive side refuse to acknowledge it. We have not reached Nirvana and more progress needs to be made, but that progress is likely to be more rapid if we focus on the great achievements in race relations that we have seen rather than the negative occurrences that inevitably occur among imperfect human beings.

We each have spheres of influence that we should use to cultivate more harmony in racial matters. That means when topics arise that are related to race, we should chime in with positive comments rather than stand with our heads down in the corner and hope not to be noticed. We must push back against the narrative that we live in a systemically racist nation that is only concerned about maintaining a white power structure. Such narratives certainly are effective in stimulating animosity and charges of unfairness, but as we have seen in previous chapters, they are blatantly false. Marxist regimes virtually always divide and demonize people in order to create an atmosphere that demands change. Their views would never be entertained by people who are content and hopeful about their future. By condemning America and our whole system that is based around individual freedom, those who want to fundamentally change our nation are planting the seeds that they hope will germinate into their "idyllic" government-run society.

When I think of my group of friends, I think of them as individuals and not as members of a particular ethnic group. I think that if anyone does an honest analysis of their own attitudes, they will find that they don't put their friends in racial boxes that determine how they are treated. Your true friends are your friends because of who they are and not because of their external appearance. Once you get to really know someone, all of their peripheral manifestations are subjugated to their true identity. I believe most Americans understand this, and a lot of the racial tension that we have seen lately is the result of successful agitators raising doubts about who we actually are as Americans. We should reject them and return to our Judeo-Christian values, which tell us to love our neighbors. That command does not apply only to the neighbors who agree with you. We must come to the recognition that everyone has different life experiences, which cause them to see things differently. Life would be very boring if everyone else agreed with you about everything. It would also be less than desirable if everybody looked exactly like you. We should be grateful for variety.

So how do we move forward in a nation that has been

accused of all types of racial transgressions? One of the first things we must do is stop looking for a racial angle in every conflict. When I became the secretary of HUD, the left-wing media were relentless in their search for something to criticize. Initially they settled on a story about the need to replace the dilapidated and dangerous dining furniture in the secretary's office complex. They claimed that I was purchasing expensive furniture while at the same time cutting the budget on disenfranchised Americans. The seventeen-piece dining room set, which was never purchased, by the way, was priced at $31,000. That happens to be a very reasonable price for quality wood furniture, which the media knew, but they saw an opportunity to try to damage me by distorting the story and claiming that a single table was being purchased at that cost. The real irony here is that it would be difficult for me to care less about furniture. It is something that has never been of interest to me and probably never will be. At any rate, the inspector general carried out an investigation at a taxpayer cost of nearly $1 million. The investigation showed no wrongdoing on my behalf, but interestingly the left-wing media that had been calling for my resignation had absolutely nothing to say. The next tactic they employed to try to damage me was saying that my family was heavily involved in the affairs of HUD and that my wife even had an office in the building. An almost $2 million IG investigation showed nothing, which of course came as no surprise to me since I knew there was nothing to find.

Some people would have seen all this as racial harassment, but the fact is the left-wing media made an all-out attempt to damage many Trump appointees and this was more of a political witch hunt than anything else. I will admit, however, that the left-wing media and the progressive politicians have a particular disdain for conservative Blacks who refuse to be constrained by left-wing ideology. If there is a form of systemic racism, it exists among the political class that thinks they have the right to determine how Black people should think. Why should there be a Black way to think any more than there should be a white way to think? It is imperative that Black people start thinking for themselves and not be subjected to manipulation by scheming, power-hungry politicians who tell them what they must believe or punish them by proclaiming them an Uncle Tom or a race traitor. They certainly have used those terms and worse when referring to me, but fortunately I find my comfort zone in my relationship with God.

If we are going to move the ball down the field with respect to racial relationships in America, we must abandon the idea that all white people are oppressors. This is one of the most ridiculous charges ever leveled against any group in our nation. The vast majority of white people never owned slaves and never had the power or desire to reengineer our society in a way to establish and preserve white power. Were there some who did have that desire and power? The answer is yes, there absolutely were such individuals, but it is patently unfair to accuse millions of people of something carried out by relatively few of their members. White people in America must understand that they are being manipulated into a position of guilt that makes it much easier to steer them in the direction of ideological political moves like defunding the police, releasing convicted criminals prematurely, and neglecting border security, to name a few. I must keep returning to the theme that people are people. There are good white people and bad white people. There are good Black people and bad Black people. There are good Asian people and bad Asian people. I think you get the point. We cannot persist with the escalation of identity politics if we are to have peace in a multicultural and multiethnic nation. Stoking the fires of division based on racial identity is a no-brainer for the forces that wish to divide and conquer. We cannot let them prevail.

The forces of division are master manipulators. One of their genius members was Saul Alinsky. He was a self-described community organizer who was also a friend of Al Capone. In his book *Rules for Radicals*, he outlined the techniques that should be used for societal change without the need for traditional political consensus. He and the Marxists advocate for the use of the masses in order to accomplish their goals. Many of the people they use, they actually despise, and refer to them as "useful idiots." They are clearly using white guilt and Black victimhood to their advantage as they attempt to radically change America. Only when the

American people understand how they are being manipulated will they be able to identify and resist the perpetrators of the destruction of the American dream. I would suggest going to the library and reading *Rules for Radicals*, in order to better understand the adversary. We the American people must come to an understanding that we are not each other's enemies simply because we have different opinions about things. We have an amazing country that is the envy of the world, but we are letting those who hate America convince us otherwise. I think if you go on a search for a better country, you will quickly recognize the gem that we have here.

As we mentioned earlier, there are a lot more things that bring us together than things that separate us. Even when we think about the lands of origin of our ancestors, whether they be England or a country in Africa or Ireland or France or Italy or Brazil, we still as Americans share a much closer common bond with each other through our own unique blended heritage. It is always refreshing when we are traveling abroad to hear another American accent and quickly become acquainted with our fellow Americans.

It is not uncommon, depending on the season, for the conversation to quickly turn to sports and particularly football. There was a time when friendly rivalries provided a great deal of enjoyment. Now many people refuse to watch NFL games because of the bitterness injected into an all-American pastime by the act of kneeling when the national anthem is played. Some teams have avoided the controversy by keeping the players hidden until afterward.

I think many of the kneeling athletes are good people, but they do not realize that they are being manipulated to divide the American people. If they really are concerned about Black lives and police brutality, I hope they will consider going to Chicago and other cities where there is great violence and using their celebrity influence to bring the police and the community together. A couple of NFL athletes kneeling at the site of a teenage murder and praying would be a powerful image, and if it was repeated several times, I have no doubt that it would have an impact and some lives would be saved. They could also ride along with the police to gain some perspective on the dangers of police work. I have no problem with protests. They are a part of the glorious freedom afforded to all American citizens. But we would do well to analyze whether those protests are doing anything useful or are further dividing the country.

In Singapore, even though there was a lot of government control, I think the healing balm was that people from different racial groups and religions were able to spend time together and to get to know each other. This has resulted in one of the most peaceful mixed societies on the planet. As we look for further ways to improve racial harmony in America, I think we would be well advised to look at Singapore's example. We still have a significant amount of racial segregation in church congregations. Some congregations have begun the practice of planned mixed social gatherings. These gatherings give birth to many healthy friendships and a natural integration of church services without the need for government intervention and oversight. In Singapore the actions that were taken were deliberate and targeted. We can do the same thing here, but the government does not have to be involved.

Another way to move forward involves a nonpolitical look at police/community relations. The police must be willing to take a serious look at nonlethal methods for restraining uncooperative people, and communities must be willing to actually look at the data regarding police brutality and admit that there have historically been some misstatements of the facts. Police should always be equipped with and use their body cameras, and there should not be long delays in releasing the footage when controversial cases arise. Giving the public access to the actual police calls and allowing the public to actually see the police in action will undoubtedly create much more sympathy and understanding for what they have to face every day.

When policies that were perhaps not discriminatory in their origin still manage to discriminate against protected groups, we have something known as disparate impact. When public schools are funded via the local tax base, many minority students are negatively impacted because they live in neighborhoods that do not enjoy a high tax base because the incomes of the inhabitants of those communities are low. Such students do not have access to the best equipment or facilities, which makes their emergence from a disadvantaged environment considerably less likely.

This perpetuation of poor education and thus poverty was perhaps not intended, but it is a stubborn fact that needs to be dealt with. It is easy for those who want to fundamentally change our nation to cultivate envy and even hatred when the facilities used to educate our children are so drastically different. This is a local issue that must be dealt with by local and state governments. When this issue is finally addressed, I believe it will make a big positive difference in race relations.

Compassion is something that is not lacking in American society. We have many organizations designed to help those in need. Unfortunately, they tend to be scattered all over any given metropolitan area, making access to them very difficult for the people who need them the most. This is the reason that EnVision Centers were created during my time at HUD. We were able to combine the efforts of thirteen federal agencies with state and local agencies as well as nonprofits and faith-based organizations all under the same roof in an effort to facilitate the climb from poverty and dependency to self-sufficiency. For instance, in some of the EnVision Centers, a single mom with three little ones could gain access to childcare while she was completing her GED, if necessary, or could receive further training that would allow her to become self-sufficient and, more important, teach self-sufficiency to her children. This is the way the cycle of poverty can be thwarted. I have visited several of the centers and witnessed fabulous collaborative efforts among the many agencies and groups working side by side to put vulnerable Americans on a trajectory of success. Hopefully the new administration will see the value of the centers and expand on the effort. Focusing on how to enhance these kinds of efforts will provide much more value to our society than concentrating on perceived or actual injustice.

Another program that was developed during my time at HUD was the Find Shelter tool. We have all encountered people who live on the streets and often don't know where their next meal is coming from. Many of them are suffering from drug addiction or mental illness, and they are certainly deserving of our compassion. There are more than seven thousand organizations that provide shelter or food or other essentials to homeless people in America. These places are not always easy to locate, especially for someone who may have educational or mental issues. We developed a QR code that can be found in many public places and scanned with a smartphone to provide a list of local organizations that will provide people experiencing homelessness with many of the necessities for their survival and comfort. The same information can also be accessed on the web at HUD.gov/findshelter.

Perhaps one of the biggest challenges that we must overcome as a nation is the perception that we are each other's enemies. There was a time in America when we helped each other gladly regardless of religion or political beliefs. Now because of the manipulation that has been so successful, we have a situation where neighbors become enemies because they have different yard signs. I suspect that you could take the most left-wing liberal and the most right-wing conservative and find that they agree on 90 percent of things. The problem is that the 10 percent on which they don't agree has been magnified and distorted by those who are attempting to divide the nation. We must remember that in many cases the person with the different yard sign has lived peacefully across the street from you for twenty years with no problems.

Instead of getting in our respective corners and demonizing each other, we need to be encouraging in-depth conversations that will in most cases show us that there is common ground upon which to build a harmonious relationship. I have also found that by engaging in conversation that is nonaccusatory, nonconfrontational, and factually based, many people who perhaps once fitted into the category of useful idiots begin to see the light, and I have seen some significant conversions. What we must remember is that we live in a diverse nation with diverse ideas. Our symbol is the bald eagle, which soars majestically above the mountains and the plains because it has two wings: a right wing and a left wing. It will not be able to gain liftoff if it has two right wings or two left wings, and it certainly will not be able to soar that way. Is there a lesson there for us as a nation that wants to soar?

The whole concept of political correctness and "woke"-ism is antithetical to the principles of our founding. These entities constrain both our speech and our actions while a complicit government looks on. Until recently, I could not remember a time when Americans were afraid to express themselves due to the possibility of cancellation or other punitive measures. When we allow social media and big companies to dictate what we can and cannot say and to mandate what we can and cannot do, we are opening the door to dictatorship.

In order for a totalitarian government to gain the necessary authority for total domination, it must first insinuate itself into every aspect of the lives of the people. Initially this is done by creating dependency. This means offering free medical care, subsidized shelter, subsidized food, free higher education and preschool, along with a host of other perks to which people quickly become addicted. Once people feel that they cannot survive without the government's assistance, they are hooked and can be easily controlled by the sugar daddy government. Over time the goodies diminish as resources are overtaxed, but the now established way of doing things must be maintained in many cases by the use of force. This is historically how you change from a free society to a totalitarian society.

You don't have to be terribly observant to see that we are moving in that direction. Racial animus is just one of the tools being used to guide us away from liberty and justice for all and to government guidance and enforcement for all. It is important to remember that the government is not necessarily evil, but rather acts as all governments do, which is to grow and infiltrate and control the populace.

Our founders were students of history and were very aware of the fact that governments naturally move toward more control and less freedom. This is the reason that they worked so long and hard on our Constitution. It was to be the tool used by the people to preserve their freedom. That tool, however, can only be utilized by a courageous populace that has read and understands it.

According to the Declaration of Independence, the people have the right to change the government if it becomes unresponsive and is not working for them. The Constitution is there to help them in that process, but more importantly, to keep us from reaching the point where that kind of change is necessary. Fascism is now a real threat to the United States because it combines the power of the private sector with that of the government to achieve predetermined goals.

An example would be government rewards to companies that punish individuals who refuse to be vaccinated for COVID-19 even though they may have natural immunity, which is better than the immunity conferred by the vaccine. That same government through taxes and penalties punishes companies that refuse to do its bidding. What is truly frightening about the COVID-19 scenario is the government's refusal to acknowledge natural immunity and the numerous studies that have shown how effective it is against the virus. This kind of "do as I say and keep your mouth shut" mentality drives those who are reluctant to get the vaccination further into their corners of resistance.

History shows us that in those kinds of cases, Marxist regimes demonize the group that is not cooperating, then impose restrictions on them, and then levy fines and penalties, and we certainly have much historical evidence of what comes after that. That is why it is so important to recognize the signs of impending totalitarianism and to take steps to avert it before it is too late. Again, I would emphasize that we currently probably do not have a Marxist government in place, but we need to be very careful to make sure that remains the case.

There are a few more things that we should consider as we move along the forward path. One of them involves elections. Fair elections are a cornerstone of a functional democratic republic. It is not adequate to simply say our elections are fair and you should not talk about them. It is also not reasonable to just complain about unfairness and not do anything about it. Of critical importance to the future of our nation is agreement upon what is and is not fair, as well as transparency in the process of voting.

Having observers who are so far away from the people who are handling the ballots that they can't see what's going on makes no sense. Not requiring signature matches makes no sense. Allowing people to vote from two different places or counting the votes of people who are deceased makes no sense. Utilizing voting machines that are accessible through the internet makes no sense. I would like to see someone try to defend any of those things.

What we need to do is convene a bipartisan congressional

panel to address these issues on an urgent basis. The longer we allow doubt, the more carnage we will have to deal with. We also need to deal with the length of service of our elected officials as well as some of our appointed officials. When our nation was established, it was anticipated that representatives would only serve for a short time and then return to their communities. Instead, we now have many career politicians who have been in Washington in excess of three decades. Some of them are doing a fine job, but that doesn't mean that there are not others in their district who could also do a fine job on a much shorter-term basis. Members of Congress are constantly engaged in fund-raising for the next run as opposed to concentrating on the business of the people. Perhaps it is time to consider a much longer term, like eight, ten, or twelve years, where the people don't have the ability to recall the representative every two years.

As far as some federal judgeships, including the Supreme Court, are concerned, when it was decided that they should have lifetime appointments, the average life span was less than fifty years. Now we are looking at eighty years, and it could possibly expand beyond that. There is certainly nothing wrong with reevaluating one's posture when circumstances change.

Everyone needs health care at some point during their lives. Health care may not be a right, but it certainly is a responsibility of a caring society. The United States spends more on health care than any other nation in the world.

Currently our annual health care spending is approaching $4 trillion, or more than $11,000 per person.[1] This should tell us that there is something wrong. We have not focused on the most efficient and effective methods of health care distribution. We have a system that does not necessarily encourage personal responsibility, and we have a massive bureaucracy that interferes with doctor-patient relationships. It is not necessary to reinvent the wheel since there are several nations around the world that deliver good health care more efficiently than we do. We could easily extract the best components of each of those systems and add a component of personal responsibility, such as one sees in health savings accounts, to rectify the problem. Like immigration and border control, it's too juicy of a political issue for Congress to actually solve. Until we have a majority of true solution-oriented leaders, this problem will languish in the bins of neglect.

There are several other areas that we could discuss as we consider the path forward to a more harmonious nation, but a good understanding of how this nation operates politically is necessary in order to prioritize. An enormous amount of power resides within each of the agencies of the federal executive branch. These agencies have both political appointees and career appointees. Career appointees are frequently there for many decades and drive a lot of policies or impede policies with which they disagree. Because the majority of career government workers reside in the Washington, DC, area, they tend to reflect

Washington, DC, political thinking. This informs the way they approach their jobs. For this reason, it is perhaps time to start considering moving some of the federal agencies to different parts of the country so that one gets a more representative group of people working on policies that affect everyone. This is not to complain about the people who are currently in place but rather simply to suggest a more representative method of governing.

In this book, we have discussed a long list of topics that have implications for racial relationships as well as for the optimal functioning of our society. Yes, we do still have some racial issues in our country, but things are a thousand times better than they used to be. That does not mean that we shouldn't strive for even better relationships, but I think those will be achieved more quickly if we work together without demonizing each other than if we try to achieve our goals by creating guilt and victimhood.

The United States remains the pinnacle nation of the world, although we've taken some severe body blows lately. If we are to thrive in the future, we must be able to concentrate on critical issues like energy independence, equality of opportunity for all, adherence to our Constitution, protection of our electrical grid, care for those who cannot care for themselves, border security, mounting debt, space domination, economic growth, national safety, environmental stability, and election integrity. These things are not in order of importance, but they are all very important, along with several other things that we could mention.

If we neglect these issues and instead spend time fighting each other, we are doomed to failure.

Perhaps it is time for us to harken back to when we actually believed what is written on every coin in our pocket and every bill in our wallet: "In God We Trust." God has favored our nation because we tried to honor Him. Observing godly values, like loving your neighbor and caring for the poor, as well as developing your God-given talents to the upmost, will make us more valuable to the people around us.

Finally, having values and principles that govern our lives will ensure not only harmony at home but stability around the globe. The choice is ours.

EPILOGUE

W E ARE FEARFULLY AND WONDERFULLY MADE in the image of God. That includes our magnificent brain. The human brain has billions of neurons and hundreds of billions of interconnections. It can process more than two million bits of information in one second and has the ability to recognize thousands upon thousands of different faces—even though they all contain two eyes, a nose, a mouth, and two ears. You have probably occasionally heard someone say, "Don't learn that because you will overload your brain." You cannot overload the human brain. If you learn one new fact every second, it would take you more than three million years to begin to challenge the capacity of your brain. So, with such a magnificent organ, why do we as human beings have so much trouble even with things that shouldn't matter, like the color of one's skin?

If you take a human brain and put it side by side

with an animal's brain—let's choose a dog—the surface topography is quite similar. The dog has a proportionately much bigger and more developed midbrain, which is the part that allows you to react. The human has much larger frontal lobes, which is where rational thought processing takes place. Animals react faster than people, but people are smarter than animals. This is why it is puzzling that some people are advocating that we begin to act more like animals and react to the color of a person's skin rather than use those frontal lobes to analyze the content of their character. Fortunately, we get to decide how we are going to use or not use the tremendous capacity for analysis and problem solving that we possess. I hope we don't choose the lower-level function of just reacting when so much is at stake.

ACKNOWLEDGMENTS

I would like to gratefully acknowledge the following persons without whom this book would have been very difficult:

My wonderful wife of forty-six years, Candy Carson, who did much of the research and provided much important advice.

My tremendous staff at the American Cornerstone Institute, many of whom were with me at HUD and some of whom were part of my 2016 presidential campaign.

My publishers at Hachette / Center Street who made the process easy and comfortable, especially Alex Pappas.

The millions of prayer warriors around the globe who keep us lifted up in prayer, which makes all the difference in these troubled times.

I also want to acknowledge the brave Americans who love this country and what it stands for and are willing to boldly proclaim the virtues of America and protect the rights of its citizens by using our Constitution, which was designed as a tool to help "we the people" control the insatiable appetite of government to control our lives. It is those people who are undaunted by the threats of cancellation and shaming who are the true warriors for liberty and justice for all. It is they who realize that we cannot be "the land of the free" if we are not "the home of the brave."

NOTES

Chapter 1: No One Is Born a Racist
1. "Vladimir Lenin Quotes—Page 2," AZ Quotes, www.azquotes.com/author/8716-Vladimir_Lenin?p=2.

Chapter 3: The History of Slavery and Racism in America
1. "History of the Organization of Work," *Encyclopaedia Britannica*, www.britannica.com/topic/history-of-work-organization-648000/Division-of-labour-in-the-workplace.
2. "Stele of Hammurabi Rediscovered," History.com, www.history.com/topics/ancient-history/hammurabi#section_3.
3. "America's History of Slavery Began Long Before Jamestown," History.com, www.history.com/news/american-slavery-before-jamestown-1619.
4. "Slavery in the Caribbean," Encyclopedia.com, www.encyclopedia.com/humanities/applied-and-social-sciences-magazines/slavery-caribbean.
5. "Slavery in the Caribbean," Encyclopedia.com, www.encyclopedia.com/humanities/applied-and-social-sciences-magazines/slavery-caribbean.
6. "Slavery in the Caribbean," Encyclopedia.com, www.encyclopedia.com/humanities/applied-and-social-sciences-magazines/slavery-caribbean.

7. "Adviser to Charles V," *Encyclopaedia Britannica*, www.britannica.com/biography/Bartolome-de-Las-Casas/Adviser-to-Charles-V.
8. "Slavery in the Caribbean," Encyclopedia.com, www.encyclopedia.com/humanities/applied-and-social-sciences-magazines/slavery-caribbean.
9. "America's History of Slavery Began Long Before Jamestown," History.com, www.history.com/news/american-slavery-before-jamestown-1619.
10. "What Happened to the Lost Colony of Roanoke Island?," Ancient Origins, www.ancient-origins.net/unexplained-phenomena/mysterious-lost-colony-roanoke-island-020289.
11. "How St. Augustine Became the First European Settlement in America," History.com, www.history.com/news/st-augustine-first-american-settlement.
12. "St. Augustine, Florida Is Founded," African American Registry (AAREG), https://aaregistry.org/story/st-augustine-florida-founded/.
13. "5 Myths About Slavery," History.com, www.history.com/news/5-myths-about-slavery.
14. "An Act Concerning Servants and Slaves (1705)," Encyclopedia Virginia, https://encyclopediavirginia.org/entries/an-act-concerning-servants-and-slaves-1705/.
15. "America's History of Slavery Began Long Before Jamestown," History.com, www.history.com/news/american-slavery-before-jamestown-1619.
16. "Contrabands of War," History Today, www.historytoday.com/archive/history-matters/contrabands-war.
17. "Contraband of War," Encyclopedia.com, www.encyclopedia.com/history/dictionaries-thesauruses-pictures-and-press-releases/contraband-war.
18. "The Freedmen's Colony on Roanoke Island," National Park Service, www.nps.gov/articles/the-freedmen-s-colony-on-roanoke-island.htm.
19. "The Freedmen's Colony on Roanoke Island," National Park Service, www.nps.gov/articles/the-freedmen-s-colony-on-roanoke-island.htm.
20. "5 Myths About Slavery," History.com, www.history.com/news/5-myths-about-slavery.

21. "Appomattox, Surrender At," Encyclopedia Virginia, https://encyclopediavirginia.org/entries/appomattox-surrender-at/.
22. "Abolition of Slavery Announced in Texas on 'Juneteenth,'" History.com, www.history.com/this-day-in-history/abolition-of-slavery-announced-in-texas-juneteenth.
23. "Juneteenth Independence Day 2021—Federal Holidays," FederalPay.org, www.federalpay.org/holidays/juneteenth.
24. "Reconstruction Comes to an End," History.com, www.history.com/topics/american-civil-war/reconstruction#section_4.
25. "Africans in Colonial America," NationalGeographic.org, www.nationalgeographic.org/encyclopedia/africans-colonial-america/.
26. "Jim Crow Laws Expand," History.com, www.history.com/topics/early-20th-century-us/jim-crow-laws#section_3.
27. "Civil Rights Movement," John F. Kennedy Library and Presidential Museum, www.jfklibrary.org/learn/about-jfk/jfk-in-history/civil-rights-movement.
28. "The A.G. Gaston Motel and the Birmingham Civil Rights National Monument," National Park Service, www.nps.gov/articles/ag-gaston-motel-birmingham-civil-rights-monument.htm.
29. "Southern Christian Leadership Conference," *Encyclopaedia Britannica*, www.britannica.com/topic/Southern-Christian-Leadership-Conference.
30. "Civil Rights Activist James Meredith Shot," History.com, www.history.com/this-day-in-history/james-meredith-shot.
31. "James Meredith," Biography.com, www.biography.com/activist/james-meredith.
32. "Civil Rights Activist James Meredith Shot," History.com, www.history.com/this-day-in-history/james-meredith-shot.

Chapter 5: Critical Race Theory and the 1619 Project

1. Henry Louis Gates Jr., "Did Black People Own Slaves?," *The Root*, March 4, 2013, www.theroot.com/did-black-people-own-slaves-1790895436.
2. Ron Haskins, "Three Simple Rules Poor Teens Should Follow to Join the Middle Class," Brookings Institution, March 13, 2013, www.brookings.edu/opinions/three-simple-rules-poor-teens-should-follow-to-join-the-middle-class/.

Chapter 6: The George Floyd Turning Point

1. Lia Eustachewich, "Kentucky AG Denies Cops Executed 'No-Knock Warrant' in Breonna Taylor Case," *New York Post*, September 23, 2020, https://nypost.com/2020/09/23/kentucky-ag-breonna-taylor-cops-knocked-and-announced-themselves/.
2. Noah Manskar, "Riots Following George Floyd's Death May Cost Insurance Companies Up to $2B," *New York Post*, September 16, 2020, https://nypost.com/2020/09/16/riots-following-george-floyds-death-could-cost-up-to-2b/.

Chapter 8: Does Systemic Racism Exist in America?

1. Aaron Bandler, "5 Statistics You Need to Know About Cops Killing Blacks," *Daily Wire*, July 7, 2016, www.dailywire.com/news/5-statistics-you-need-know-about-cops-killing-aaron-bandler; Heather Mac Donald, "The Danger of the 'Black Lives Matter' Movement," *Imprimis* 45, no. 4 (April 2016), https://imprimis.hillsdale.edu/wp-content/uploads/2016/05/Imprimis_April16.pdf.
2. Ian Thomsen, "1,000 People in the US Die Every Year in Police Shootings. Who Are They?," News@Northeastern, April 16, 2020, https://news.northeastern.edu/2020/04/16/000-people-in-the-us-are-killed-every-year-in-police-shootings-how-many-are-preventable/.
3. Jesse Washington, "Blacks Struggle with 72 Percent Unwed Mothers Rate," NBC News, November 7, 2010, www.nbcnews.com/id/wbna39993685.
4. Ann M. Simmons, "There Are More Slaves Now Than Any Time in Human History," *Daily News*, September 19, 2017, www.nydailynews.com/news/world/slaves-time-human-history-article-1.3506975.

Chapter 12: The Path Forward

1. "National Health Expenditure Data, Historical," Centers for Medicare & Medicaid Services, www.cms.gov/Research-Statistics-Data-and-Systems/Statistics-Trends-and-Reports/NationalHealthExpendData/NationalHealthAccountsHistorical.